THE

IMPACT
FORMULA

Powerful solutions for turbo-charging
your influence

OLIVER MEDILL

The Impact Formula

First published in 2018 by

Panoma Press Ltd
48 St Vincent Drive, St Albans, Herts, AL1 5SJ, UK
info@panomapress.com
www.panomapress.com

Book layout by Neil Coe.

Printed on acid-free paper from managed forests.

ISBN 978-1-784521-19-6

The right of Oliver Medill to be identified as the author of this work has been asserted in accordance with sections 77 and 78 of the Copyright, Designs and Patents Act 1988.

A CIP catalogue record for this book is available from the British Library.

This book is available online and in bookstores.

Dedication

For Alina

Acknowledgements

Firstly, my unreserved thanks go out to all my clients who, knowingly or otherwise, have taught me more than I will ever be able to teach them.

To the Webber Douglas Academy of Dramatic Art, unreserved thanks for showing me technique, discipline and hope when I had none.

To the old Speakers International, for giving me an unrivalled grounding in the art of public speaking, of stagecraft, of storytelling of facilitation and last but certainly not least, of understanding – in the early stages at least – just how terrified it is possible to be, and to succeed every time.

To my colleagues and friends Ben, Martin, Colin, Jim, Andrew, Andy, Simon, Paul, Adrian and Lisa my thanks to you, gurus all.

To the Ryder 8, my thanks for reminding me what life is all about.

To Simon, I will always be grateful for your unswerving support and friendship and for your honest feedback whenever I have needed it – which has been often.

To my sister Rachel, whose footsteps I have followed all my life and whose huge achievements have always spurred me on to do my best. Don't forget how it is.

To my parents – your generosity of heart has been the inspiration at the centre of everything I do.

Lastly to Alina – my rock. Thank you for putting up with me through all the travel and all the uncertainty, especially during the writing of this book.

Contents

'All things be ready if our minds be so.'

William Shakespeare

Prologue

'You lucky bastard!' – the remembered words of my best friend echo in my ears as I roll over, trying to blot out the roar of the engines outside the fuselage. 'Spare a thought for me in the office while you're swanning off round the world, sipping champagne at 40,000 feet.'

I look at the dial of my watch – 3.43am – I have to remind myself is that UK time or…? My brain's a bit muzzy.

In the last five days I have flown from London to Madrid and from there to Santiago in Chile, where I have delivered a two-hour keynote speech to an audience of partners in a global consulting firm. From there, I have left the stage, jumped into a taxi to the airport and immediately flown to Dubai, via Madrid once more. A panicked two-hour change from one airline to another, then seven more hours flying to Dubai and an arrival at 4am. Yet another taxi to my hotel, five hours of desperately needed sleep, then another two-hour keynote speech, this time to a global pharmaceutical company.

At the end of this speech, I have to rush the Q&A and the goodbyes and run because my flight back to London leaves in three hours. Another ten hours later, we're joining the landing queue for Heathrow. After the blur of the last few days, I allow myself the luxury of looking out of the window as we float over London, before the tight turn over the reservoirs and our landing. There's an early mist and the sun's kissing the autumnal landscape with pure magic.

Food for the soul.

It's only a matter of four hours later and I'm looking down once again, this time on the west coast of Ireland, as we head out across the Atlantic, bound for California and my third speech in my third continent in a week. At San Francisco, just the walk from the airport building to the taxi reminds me that there is a 20 degree temperature change from London – it's totally different here.

An hour's drive later, I am awakened from a coma-like sleep as we arrive at the hotel, where my presentation is taking place the next morning. I'm running on empty, even as I am reminded as I check in that there's a welcome reception and some networking in an hour's time, followed by a dinner…

'Good afternoon sir and welcome to the Ritz Carlton, San Francisco. How are you doin' today?'

I do my best but only manage a lopsided smile that is more of a grimace, as she gets a curt nod instead.

The evening passes in a blur and even though I get a desperately needed few hours of sleep later, my body clock is somewhere in the Middle East, so I am exhaustedly awake again while it's still dark outside. A couple of positive thoughts: Just one more to go, Oliver, and then you've got three weeks before you have to travel again.

Once again, the speech – a 90-minute look at resilience – goes down well and before I know it, I'm wandering through duty free, once more at the airport and this time homeward bound. I've flown over 30,000 miles in less than a week. I'm honestly not sure where I am, *when* I am, or how I am still functioning, whilst feeling this tired.

'Lucky bastard?' I grin wryly at the thought.

But my odyssey isn't quite over. As I sit in the airport lounge awaiting the call for my flight, a polite voice enquires if the seat next to me is taken. I smile perfunctorily and next to me sits down the gentleman who changes my life…

Introduction

The Lost Man

I was working as an office manager in a financial services company. I hated it. I didn't understand the ins and outs of this particular set of products, nor did I want to. Each day that passed filled me with a terrible sense of waste. I had a degree in modern languages but I didn't want to teach. I had learned how to cook, but I didn't want to be a chef. I knew that I had a creative streak, but advertising didn't really do it for me and I couldn't say that any ideas I had had to date had really excited me enough for me to make any serious life changes.

The only thing I really enjoyed was my latest hobby, the local amateur dramatics society, three evenings a week. We were putting on *A Chorus of Disapproval* by Alan Ayckbourn, in which I had a lead role, which was great fun and a much needed escape valve for the frustration, apathy and boredom of my day-to-day existence.

Whilst I loved the acting, I was painfully aware that to be any good I needed training – and lots of it. Sadly, having been to university had scuppered any chance of getting a grant for one of the reputable drama schools, which were famously expensive, so I was forced to put up with the existing status quo and to see the possibility of being an actor for what it was – a pipe dream.

Things came to a head one Friday afternoon as I was trundling back into London on the tube, after a particularly painful seminar on offshore bonds at a dreary Heathrow conference centre. I was at an all-time low; we had just had our performance of *A Chorus of Disapproval*, where my efforts had been surprisingly well received. This, of course, had only made things worse; the acting was all the more seductive when compared to my utter misplacement in my current job – and all the more tantalisingly out of reach.

I looked out of the window at the grey landscape, thinking about my grey life, and I remember swearing to myself that if only I had the money, I would leave my job within the hour and go straight to drama school without passing GO!

I arrived back at the office and there were two messages from my mother to phone her. It seemed that a recently departed uncle I had met twice in my life had left me enough money in his will for me to go to drama school.

Extraordinary! Things like this only happen in Hollywood! Life could begin anew.

I left my job within the hour.

Of course, I didn't realise at the time that one actually had to get *in* to drama school; places were hugely contested and the audition process was rigorous, to say the least. But fate, it seemed, was on my side. There was an audition slot a week away at my preferred school, The Webber Douglas Academy of Dramatic Art, and if by great good fortune I were to win a place, the first term was due to start a mere six weeks away.

And so, after a frankly terrifying day in front of some theatrical luminaries, who remained grimly inscrutable in face of my efforts (such as they were), I was curtly informed I would hear by post within a week.

Despite this rather inauspicious experience, I duly received my much longed-for offer of a place. I will always remember opening the letter and the feeling of pure joy that flooded through me as I read the words 'we are delighted to offer you…' It made all the dark days of the past worthwhile. And what's more, I finally knew what it was like to have a sense of vocation, to have real hope for the future, to feel that I was, for the first time, doing what I was truly passionate about.

And yes, of course there were challenges that lay ahead, not the least of which were (and still are for that matter) the appalling statistics of success in this, the most beguiling of industries: over 75% of actors earn less than £5,000 a year; only the top 2% of actors make £20,000 or more a year. And yet somehow none of this mattered. In a way, it made the struggle ahead seem even more exciting.

The next two years passed in a happy blur of attempting to get rid of bad habits, classes on improvisation, Shakespeare, movement, voice training, dance, stage fighting, huge amounts of stark and very public criticism from frankly terrifying teachers, culminating in full-blown performances to audiences of agents, casting directors and producers. And somewhere in the midst of all this there was a slowly growing professional competence in an ancient craft, together with a sense of pride to belong – as however tiny a cog – to this extraordinarily colourful profession.

Fast Forward Seven Years

I was still searching. Whilst I had been lucky and I landed more work than most of my actor friends, I was now a (largely) unemployed actor, cooking dinners and lunches as a means to pay the rent. I had discovered that being an actor was not about acting. It was about *resilience*. Living with rejection and feeling OK about it.

Picture the scene: Once in a while, let's say every two or three weeks, my agent would call me with a time and a place for my next audition. It might be for theatre, TV, film or commercial work. She would tell me where to go and when and I would duly trot off at the appointed time to the studios, normally in Soho or the West End, tucked away off Oxford Street. I would ring the buzzer, go up a few flights, and there, in an annexe, would typically sit between six and ten men of either very or vaguely similar casting size and age as myself.

My competition. A fascinating study in human behaviour. Some of them I would see regularly and there would be a rather tired exchange of wry smiles. A couple of them would already be 'in character', assuming an air of complete indifference (we were always told to pretend we didn't care if we got the job or not and then blow them away with the audition itself) – although I knew all too well the feeling... the inner chat... ('Oh no! HE's here. He was really good in that thing on BBC2 the other night – they're bound to pick him' etc.). There would also inevitably be a motley sprinkling of flamboyant clothing: fedoras, waistcoats, even cravats on occasion.

Eventually, I would get called into a room where there would be seated the usual trio: casting director, director and producer. I would have been sent a couple of pages of the script in advance and would know the lines backwards, although I would never dream of telling them this. The trick was to hold the script in my hand as if I had only just seen it, so I could then 'wow' them with my 'impromptu' performance. There would be a perfunctory shaking of hands and 'thanks for coming ins' before a brief introduction and setting of context by either director or producer.

The immortal line, 'whenever you're ready…' and I would deliver my version of the next police inspector, or Shakespearean villain, or washing powder strapline, or sitcom character.

'That's great, thanks!' Smiles all round, out I would go, massaging cheeks that by this time would be aching from too much forced smiling, on with the coat and I would be walking down the pavement to Oxford Street tube, just an ordinary guy again, but with the hope burning bright of a call from my agent with the good news.

One of the hardest things to handle as an actor is the outdated and very cruel practice that, having been to an audition and 'laid it on the line', you would have a one in ten chance of bagging the part. On the other hand, a potentially never-ending wait for the phone to ring. If you didn't get the part, they would never tell you.

What a profession! Tailor made for neurotics.

So, I was lucky – I had a great agent and I did some good stuff: a year-long engagement, straight out of drama school, in a national tour and West End run of *Hamlet* in a good role; a run of nice character parts in well-known and long-running British dramas (*Soldier Soldier, Silent Witness, The Bill, Hornblower, Sword of Honour, Heartbeat* etc.); some lucrative commercials for TV and even a couple of movie parts.

I was doing better than most actors out there and for the lean times (most of the time) I had a means of paying my rent as a cook, a skill learnt in France during my year's placement at university.

I should have been happy – and I felt lost. Once again.

My career was being decided by other people; there was absolutely no control, no ability to make plans (what if I were to get an audition?), no ability to put down roots (mortgage companies were funny about giving money to people with no job security), and what was more, I had a sneaking suspicion that making a living pretending to be someone else wasn't very good for me. I mean, how the hell was I supposed to understand others if I didn't know who *I* was?

The Lifeline

The phone hadn't rung for over a month and whilst I had a couple of cooking jobs lined up, there was a nasty habit of watching daytime TV building up and whilst I was going through the motions, I was struggling for balance. It was a normal morning. Absent-mindedly I flopped down on to the sofa.

An advert came on to the TV screen. It was a guy called Anthony Robbins, talking about a 30-day audio CD programme which will 'change your life'. So as we know, I had kind of been there and done that and have a drawer full of T-shirts. But once a frustrated dreamer, always a frustrated dreamer… so I listened.

The clincher for me (money being in short supply) was that it was an 'if you don't like it, send it back and we'll charge you nothing' product. So, I signed up and a few days later a large parcel arrived, complete with a journal and 30 days' worth of CDs.

It remained one of my best ever decisions. I casually slotted in one of the CDs, pressed play… and everything changed. Very quickly I was sold on the concepts that the past doesn't equal the future and that I had the personal power to change my life for the better.

My path was set, once again. I made some changes to my beliefs about myself and about the world around me. I learned about some of the habitual behaviours that were really limiting my growth and potential. I also learned some strategies that really worked for me. There was a spring in my step; I had purpose and self-belief and very quickly the people around me noticed a profound difference.

I realised that the sense of purpose and self-belief was something that I wanted to focus on as a career. I also realised that I had absolutely no credibility or experience in this world, so my first step was to get some. (Sound familiar?)

I duly studied and gained qualifications in performance coaching and also Neuro Linguistic Programming (NLP), as well as certification in group dynamics from the brilliant Michael Grinder. I am sure you've heard the saying 'when the student is ready, the teacher will appear'.

As if by magic, three days after receiving my final qualification, one of my great friends, an event organiser, told me that she had used this speaker agency for one of her conferences and she thought I could do a better job than the guy she had hired, which I thought was extremely generous seeing as she'd never seen me on my feet. Nonetheless, she also gave me the contact number and I duly put in a call.

I went in for a chat and I quickly found out that, whilst extremely pressurised, this was a highly desirable (and contested) position in an aspirational industry and, as a result, the interview process was rigorous to say the least. More than once, my confidence was badly shaken as I was compelled to jump through the hoops of no fewer than five interviews. However, persistence paid off, it would seem, and many bumps in the road later, I started my speaking career for an international speakers agency.

The Learning Curve

My time at the international agency was hugely important. This was the time that theory turned rather brutally into practice. I learned that it was one thing to read a book about public speaking, but it was quite another to be literally shoved on stage.

Picture this:

The phone on my desk rang – it was Dave.

'I've got a gig for you in Northamptonshire, starting tomorrow,' he said. 'Three keynote speeches on three consecutive days for three different audiences – same topic.'

'What's the topic?' I asked.

'It's their annual "ra-ra",' he said, 'they're calling it "search for the hero" and they want a 90-minute keynote speech on belief systems, with a glass walk at the end.'

'Er, by "glass walk" do you mean the bit at the end, where I ask people to come up on stage and get them to walk over broken glass in their bare feet?'

'That's the one,' he said.

'But I've never done a glass walk,' I protested. 'How many in the audience?'

'Three thousand,' he said, 'but that's divided into three for the three days, so it's only a thousand per speech.'

'Oh excellent,' I said, not feeling it, 'and how do you propose I learn this glass walk?'

'Not really my problem,' he chortled, 'I'm just the sales guy,' and then more seriously, 'look, it's really easy – just go and ask Alan, he's done loads of them.'

Alan was running a workshop for a client on mental toughness for the day, but I did have half an hour on the phone with him that evening, when he talked me through the 'dos and don'ts' of the 'metaphor', or call to action, which was this mysterious 'glass walk'.

The following day, I had driven to Northamptonshire and had met the clients who were 'expecting big things' and apparently I had 'big shoes to fill'. It turned out that my predecessor, who had left the company for a career in teaching, had 'wowed' the audience the year before.

I still hadn't actually taken anyone through this exercise, as I stood in the wings of the auditorium, about to be introduced as the guest speaker. What made things spectacularly worse was that the speech I had prepared had been instantly dismissed when the client had seen my proposed slides. Apparently there were 'too many similarities to last year – if you do this stuff, they'll eat you alive.'

I might have had half an hour's sleep at a push and I was trying to remember the main points of the new speech – a hastily cobbled together alternative piece of content that I had barely learnt in my four months with the company.

As for the 'glass walk', I had managed to reconcile myself to taking sound advice and relying on the physics of mass + breaking glass – oh, and a lot of luck – to get me through this.

As I was introduced, I tottered out on to the stage…

Now if you are thinking, ah, but you were an actor, it must have been a doddle, I would ask you consider the difference between performing in front of audiences whilst pretending to be someone else versus speaking in front of audiences *as yourself* – a quite different and in some ways a more challenging proposition.

Firstly, if you are looking to train as an actor, you *have* to know your craft. Whilst I knew that acting was the only thing I had ever enjoyed, I also knew that without the necessary acting skills I might as well not bother. I knew nothing about the technical side (for example, 'blocking'; 'upstage' versus 'downstage', or even 'centre stage' for that matter), let alone the finer points and learnt techniques connected with dramatic performance.

At drama school, they (by 'they' I mean the terrifying faculty of acting) first 'break you down' (getting rid of all your 'amateur' bad habits; it took me three terms for example to learn how to *stand,* before we even got started on breathing!), then they hammer classic technique into you.

Improvisation (*'I don't believe you!'* they would roar); 'Stanislavski's Method' (*'I don't believe you!'* they would roar); comic timing (*'Get off, you're boring!'* they would roar); the stage whisper (*'I can't hear you!'* they would roar) and so on.

Acting is all about characterisation: you learn to interpret a character firstly by reading the lines, you improvise, you process the character from the inside out and you form an impression. You focus on becoming someone else. My acting mentor's favourite line was 'you have to learn to "inhabit" a character, not just borrow their coat.' It was all terrifying, frustrating and hopelessly addictive.

As an actor, you are introspective and focusing on yourself rather than your audience; then and only then can you start to project your character and interact with the other characters in the scene. The audience just comes to watch; if you've got it right, it will work. If you haven't, it won't.

On the other side of the coin, when speaking in public in front of an audience *as yourself,* you've got to know what you're talking about, you can't just learn lines. (Well you can, but that's a sure way to fall flat on your face.)

When you speak from a professional point of view, the audience is 'bespoke' – it comes because *you're* there, either singly as a subject matter expert, or as a speaker among other speakers. Either way, your audience is there to listen, learn and form an opinion, based upon the content of your speech. Unlike inhabiting a character, your focus is – or *should* be – your audience.

There are similarities as well.

Similarly, in the world of professional speaking, you can't just rock up with a story and expect to 'wow' audiences (even though I have seen many motivational speakers do just that, with exactly those expectations and fairly dire results). You have to work on every aspect, from structure, to visual aids, to stance, posture, movement and speech.

But perhaps the biggest similarity between communicating a character from the stage and communicating *you* from the stage is founded upon a very simple process.

The Need for Rehearsal

It is normal for actors to rehearse and then rehearse some more – no play is performed without huge amounts of rehearsal because it stands to reason that to make a performance sing, you need to practise it.

When it comes to public speaking, for some reason, rehearsal seems to get pushed to the back of the queue, bypassed, or omitted altogether. I have lost count of the number of senior executives who arrive at a conference, hand their memory stick of slides to the technical team and announce to the world at large, 'I'm much better when I don't rehearse'…

Terrifying! For all the wrong reasons.

I worked as a fully–employed speaker for nearly six years, delivering speeches and workshops to audiences ranging in size from 15 to 5,000, week in, week out. After the first year, I was battle hardened enough to know the tricks which worked and the tricks which didn't. It was the school of hard knocks, where I was exposed pretty much all the time. There was no comfort zone.

I was still very green as far as tips, tricks, nuances and winning an audience over was concerned, however. It was very much a case of being consistently thrown into the deep end and having to sink or swim. My appointed supervisor, whose job it was to sit at the back from time to time and to give feedback at the end, had a nasty habit of snatching my diligently prepared notes out of my shaking hands moments before I stepped on stage and sending me off with the always remembered words 'get into state and enjoy it – you know it already.'

'Getting into state' was a phrase that he trotted out all the time, and all during that first year I was never entirely sure what he meant. I was certainly 'in *a* state' most of the time. Of course, he knew all too well the importance of a resourceful emotional state – that our emotional state controls our behaviour and consequently our performance, but I wish he had explained this more clearly at the time. It would have saved me lots of sleepless nights.

In the end, I would have a spare set of notes written on cards that he never knew about. I never used these notes of course and they always remained in my pocket, but to me they represented a 'comfort blanket' that seemed to make a difference to my ability to perform under pressure.

His behaviour was all coming from 'a good place' I'm sure, but the school of hard knocks it was and it was only after three years of living this high-pressure existence and finally understanding through experience what 'getting into state' really meant that I developed any sense of comfort on stage.

Now you may feel that this is counterproductive – i.e. why on earth would I relate the personal experience of three years of 'the school of hard knocks' before feeling OK about public speaking?!

My answer is simple: my experience will help your experience. I am 100% confident that I can turn your emotions around public speaking from what may be anxiety into total enjoyment, by following the steps outlined over the next chapters.

The Legacy

But this book isn't about me – it's about you. And I'm here to tell you, if you don't know it already, that *you* are here for a very good reason as well.

There's an old saying that goes 'we read to know we're not alone'. I hope that if you have read about my journey and you find some similarities with your own life – not necessarily about acting or the specifics of my story but more about the search for meaning and purpose, for finding where your true chance of greatness lies – that what now follows will resonate with you.

My lessons from the journey described are as follows:

- I learned that the power of change lies within us all

- I learned that a simple daily process will build fantastic habits

- I learned that most people mistakenly focus on the results they want, rather than perfecting the process. The journey, not the destination, is everything

- I learned that everything happens for a reason

- I learned that I, like everyone else, have unique skills and insights that are valuable to others

- I learned that if you have the courage to make changes, the universe *will* support you

I am offering you the chance to seize the moment.

Over the coming chapters, I will introduce you to a process that will enable you to express yourself with authenticity and passion about the things in your life that make you special, unique.

This book is not just about the speaking part, it's about the ability to build your own branded material that engages others, no matter what your area of expertise or experience.

And probably as important as anything else, I will introduce you to a personal development methodology that will keep you moving on a constant upwards curve, both in expertise and in results.

CHAPTER 1:
THE OPPORTUNITY

'Nothing will work unless you do.'

Maya Angelou

In this chapter I will be discussing the following four topics:

- What this book is about

- Who should read this book

- Why *you* should read this book

- What you will gain by using the tools and techniques in this book

What this book is about

The essence of the book revolves around the following three areas:

1. A methodology for distilling your skills, knowledge and experience into marketable content that is easy to learn, easy to follow and easy to teach.

2. The development of you, the reader, into a world-class speaker and communicator, looking at specialised techniques that will take your ability to inspire and motivate others to a whole new level.

3. It ensures that you are focusing on *growth* mentality: the critical importance of having the right mindset, self-belief, persistence and self-awareness to succeed. In addition, there is strong focus on all the necessary tools at your fingertips to ensure unstoppable confidence – whatever the situation – that will enable you to create the habit of self-development as a result.

Who should read this book

Self-employed individuals, SME owners, entrepreneurs, teachers, trainers, coaches and anyone engaged in any form of people-facing activity. In fact, if you hold any position of influence and the development of others, either explicitly as a designated leader, coach, mentor or teacher, or implicitly via the impact of sales, marketing or other people-facing disciplines, you will have specific interests, insights and experience that will be hugely valuable to others.

By harnessing the skills and techniques outlined in this book, you will be able to increase the impact of this knowledge, insights and experience on others to a level that you might not otherwise have imagined.

Why *you* should read this book

There are various reasons why people would gain from reading this book.

Do any of these questions resonate with you?

1. Whilst you are successful at what you do, are you challenged by the balance of time spent at work versus the time spent doing the irreplaceable, i.e. time with friends and family?

2. Is it the case that you've had your challenges and life has been a struggle of ups and downs, but you have always picked yourself up and have been looking for a way to channel all your effort and energy into a new and exciting future for yourself?

3. Has your big opportunity to make your mark not happened yet? Could it be that you are courageous enough to make changes in your life, but you are not entirely sure how to go about it?

4. Have you been searching for a meaningful change in one or all areas of your life and all you need is the spark and a clear path to set you on your way?

5. You hold a responsible position in your work and have great skills but might you be feeling that you're never going to break the mould and will always be an employee with a salary, whilst your company owners are making the big money?

6. Do you own your own business, but you can't seem to increase your profits, despite working incredibly hard to do so? Might it be that you need to develop other skills that will help you earn large sums of money, using expertise that you already have?

7. Do you feel that you want to reach out to a larger audience than the one you currently have – that your message/product/service will benefit more people if you reach more people?

8. Do you want to stretch yourself more – to take a whopping leap outside your comfort zone? As we know, no one grows by staying safe.

9. Are you already a good public speaker, but you want to become really great at it by improving your skills in speaking, creating compelling content and engaging the audience?

10. Or maybe you might be feeling that it's no longer enough to just be a subject matter expert? Might it be that you feel that you need to stand out from your peers with equal knowledge and know how?

11. Or is it that you feel that you want to leave a legacy?

How to make sure that this book is for you

As described, this book is aimed at a very distinct group of people. Yes, they have many different aspirations; they may well work in completely disparate industries and have little in common with one another as far as personalities go. They may want to improve their skills, reach a larger audience, make a difference and leave a legacy. They may want more work-life balance and discretionary flexibility. It may just be that they want more income.

But they all have one thing in common.

They want change.

Somewhere in your journey you have discovered that the status quo, the current situation, isn't sitting well with you. You may have even resigned yourself to living a life that hasn't quite delivered what you want. However, change is in many ways easy to understand as a necessity for improving the quality of your life, but hard to apply because whilst it offers the potential key to what you are searching for, as with everything in life worth having, it also comes at a price.

The Two Faces of Change

William Bridges, in his ground-breaking work on transitions, talks about the 'two faces of change'. This contention is at the heart of why the changes we wish to make at work or in our lives in general so often meet with failure. The answer lies in the two faces of change mentioned.

One face of change is *external* – the plans, the steps, the intent; the other is *internal* – the emotional journey that you associate with the change.

Both of these elements need to be addressed if you are going to make the life changes you want. So let's have a look at this a little closer, using an example as we go.

Example: In your world, let's be topical and imagine you want to become a public speaker around your specialist subject. You will have *external* and *internal* changes to make as a result.

Step 1 – External

In many ways, the external elements of change are the easiest ones, the specific steps needed. The external change is the nuts and bolts: the designing and writing of your content.

This will involve several planning steps; you will need to sit down and work out a structure, what needs to be in there and in what order and what style. Then you need to write it! It sounds easy, but the external side of writing content takes discipline, attention to detail and, always, the need to keep at least one foot in your audience's shoes – an ability to hear what you are writing from your audience's perspective.

Having written the content, you then need to practise your speaking skills, ask for feedback and practise like mad, before the attraction of your audience and the acid test of inspiring them even starts. So, whilst the external part of changing from subject matter expert to speaker is laborious, it is at least seen, expected and measurable.

Step 2 – Internal

The internal part of change is the unseen, often immeasurable and certainly often unexpected element.

If we continue with the change required to create content and speak with passion and credibility around it, various other elements come into play. Designing and writing content takes persistence. Being human, you may well not feel like doing this on a certain day. You may find it very difficult not to be influenced by friends and loved ones to change your approach: 'But that's not who you *are*! You should be looking to do *this* instead,' etc.

Even having got through these stages, you will then need to find the courage to step up and deliver – even when your nerve may be severely challenged. Most people deal with the rational challenges, but find real challenge with the emotional ones because the change needed isn't just about the external nuts and bolts; the change needed requires a shift in *how you see yourself.*

You cannot achieve real change in your life without taking a risk. It may be a calculated risk, but inherent in any significant change is a leap of faith, which can be scary.

The Hollywood blockbuster *Jerry Maguire* is a great example of this. Tom Cruise's character realises that he hates what his role in society has become, so he writes a mission statement from the heart, which changes the course of his life. The story is by no means plain sailing; the powers that be hate what he has written, so he loses his job, he hits rock bottom as he loses his best client, but he stays true to his dream of a better life in a better world and eventually he prevails.

Whilst this is a classic Hollywood vehicle, the story is nonetheless a great example of a parable of an inspired man who steps miles outside his comfort zone and goes on a journey. Whilst it's fictional, it's also inspirational because it's set in the modern world and is created with realism – it could be you. That's why it was such a big hit – everyone who watched it associated with the possibility of following the dream, the struggle and the final redemption.

So, whether you have been looking for a means to change for a while, or you have discovered this book by chance and want to know more about changing your life by earning money doing what you love, this chapter is about helping you to be the Jerry Maguire of your own story.

A structured approach to change

To give you structure and the commitment you will need to make your changes stick, here are the vitally important steps:

Decide   **R**ationale   **E**ngage   **A**djust   **M**odel

The first thing to do is to **D**ecide, to make a *definite decision* to change your life. It may sound simple, but it's not enough to just want to change. As Victor Kiam (the guy who liked the electric razor so much he bought the company) said, *'Procrastination is opportunity's assassin.'*

The word 'decide' comes from the Latin verb *decidere* – to cut off from. In other words, there's no grey area. You have to make a decision that is not purely rational, but that also feeds the need from your emotional brain. This can't just be a rational thing; your limbic brain, or emotional brain, controls decision making and is the boss! If it disagrees with your rational thinking, it will override rational thought and sabotage your best intentions.

To illustrate this, let's look at a great example of an individual I worked with recently.

Peter was stuck in a dead end job as he saw it. He was very much in the mould of someone who was working to live as opposed to the other way round. Living in south London with a family to feed, he had been working for a well-known telecoms company as a manager in one of their retail outlets north of the river. Days, weeks and months would pass as he endured the daily rush hour to and from north London; he would already be working hard to stay positive by the time he got into the shop because everyone looked so miserable on the tube – and this was before his day had even started!

He had lost the ability to 'enjoy the moment' in his job, where a customer would come into the shop and leave with a smile on their face. The reason? He had decided at some stage that for every happy customer there were a dozen cynics and he had lost his desire to 'convert doubt into buy-in' as his company sales manual would advise. The longer the situation lasted, the more disillusioned Peter became, until finally his wife sat him down one evening after the children had been put to bed and told him a few home truths.

'During the week, you're no longer part of this family,' was her opening line. 'I wake up with a monosyllabic stranger who no longer smiles at me, or the kids for that matter. Every evening, the same stranger plods in through the front door and grunts at us from time to time. On Friday evening, I get my husband back, until Sunday evening when the stranger returns – and I'm sick of it. Talk to me!'

Of course, this was a critical moment. Peter hadn't realised the extent to which his 'coping mechanism' had been undermining the one thing that was keeping him in his job – his love for his family. It ended up being a transformational conversation, where he opened up to his wife about his feeling of being trapped, with no way out. She, quite rightly, told him that he needed to make a clear decision either to stay in his job and make a real go of it or to find something else that would both bring in money and make him happy at the same time.

Sure enough, and true to his word, he sat down and went through all these issues, which gave him the clarity he needed to make a well-informed decision. As you may imagine, the first three questions he asked himself were both revealing and hugely thought provoking: 'How long has this thought been in my head?' 'What's missing in my life?' And especially, 'What do I want instead of the current situation?'

This allowed him to really think about his current reality versus the reality that he wanted. From the process, he realised that running a shop was not going to give him what he wanted, which was more of the people development and less of the retail.

More of Peter's story later.

So here are some steps that will get you thinking about your *real* motivators for a change rather than your *right* ones. Ask yourself some questions to create clarity of purpose.

How long has this thought been in my head?

This is a great question to ask yourself because the answer should give you some clear insights. If this is a recent discovery, then remember that changing your life doesn't have to happen immediately. You can continue to sit with the idea, and the fact that your unconscious mind is now focused upon it will give your conscious mind consistent feedback. There's a part of the brain called the Reticular Activating System, or RAS, that is a natural focus puller, in the same way that if you have a new car you suddenly become aware of the same make and model of car popping up everywhere! Does this mean that all of a sudden there are more of those cars on the road? No! It's just that your RAS makes you aware of what you are focusing on. So if you are focusing on changing your life, your day-to-day existence will be seen through the 'change' filter, produced by your RAS. If you have been thinking about change for a while, then this might be the time to take some steps.

What's missing in my life?

Again, this is a simple yet insightful question. Have a good think about what it is that is/has caused you to feel that you want this change. Be specific about the various factors involved.

What do I want instead of the current situation?

This may seem a slightly 'clunky' question but the thought behind it is profound. As humans, we are used to thinking cyclically. There is a body of research that suggests that we have approximately 60,000 thoughts a day, 90% of which are repeated daily, thereby engraining the thoughts into our habitual subconscious. Now if these thoughts are helpful, positive ones, great! What is less encouraging, however, is that an estimated 85% of the repeated daily thoughts we have are negative ones. That means that, in effect, we are our own worst enemies. Think about this scenario. Have you ever been in a meeting where something hasn't gone as well as planned and there is a moratorium going on, along the lines of: How did this happen? Who's to blame? and so on. Sound familiar?

Once again, we are culturally conditioned to behave this way, which means that the norm is a cycle of retrospective blame culture rather than a more problem-solving approach.

Asking a positive question such as, 'What do I want instead?' immediately provides proactivity and future thinking. It's like a slap in the face, which is why the technical term 'pattern interrupt' is often used for questions of this nature. The question literally forces your brain to change direction.

So in a similar way to the negative, blame-filled meeting, if you were to ask the question, 'What do we want instead?' you would immediately and completely change the focus and emotional level in the room for the better, so the same effect happens when you ask yourself a similar question about a challenge that you may have been wrestling with.

How do I know that this is worth doing?

This seemingly obvious question will provide you with specific insights into your subconscious as well as your conscious motivation.

What qualities and skills do I have that I am not using?

You may well know where your expertise lies, but asking yourself the deliberate question will force your brain to become forensic rather than generalist. We will be using this in more detail later in this chapter. List the qualities that a) you excel at and b) you love doing.

What is stopping me from changing my life around?

Whilst you may initially say to yourself 'I haven't enough time to do XYZ,' this question is really about your fears. Fear of the unknown and fear of change are perfectly natural and need to be confronted if you are to really make progress. If you ignore your perfectly natural fears of an unknown future, you will most likely procrastinate and, eventually, self-sabotage. There are six main fears that confront people. They are: Rejection, Embarrassment, Loss, Failure, Exposure and Conflict.

Again, generally the question isn't about fear of the unknown so much as fear of 'Can I do it?' and 'Will it work?' Or 'Will I get laughed at and end up looking like a fool?' and 'Can I follow through with my plan?'

How would I feel if I were still doing the same thing five years from now? What would I be saying/thinking/feeling?

Again, this is a cracking question to ask yourself, as it will give you a good emotional insight into how deeply you want your life to change. By bringing an image of the future into your consciousness, you are allowing your emotions to connect with your imagination. From asking this question and building on the three previous ones, you should have a clearer insight into your commitment levels.

Is this a want or a must?

Score on a scale of 1-10 my a) willingness and b) readiness to make changes in my life

Asking yourself to quantify your decision levels will give you clarity about your commitment levels and therefore your likelihood of success.

If your response is a resounding 10, then great! If not, ask yourself the final question:

What steps must I take to get to a 10?

In the same way that a torch beam will light up specific areas, leaving the rest in darkness, a great question which will direct your brain's torch, or focus, to solve the question you are asking.

The second thing to be clear about is the **R**ationale, or reason, for your goal – the WHY.

Many of you will be familiar with the hugely popular TED talk delivered by Simon Sinek entitled 'How great leaders inspire action'. The viral success of this 18-minute talk is due to a simple but highly effective reversal of current methods of discourse.

Age-old and standard practice when telling others about one's life and career tends to lean towards the following structure:

What: I'm a public speaker

How: I teach speaking skills to people who want to communicate better

In other words, we discuss the 'what' followed by the 'how'. The reason? It's easy! Everyone on earth knows what they do and most people know the procedures involved as well – the 'how'. But very few people consciously know *why* they do what they do. And before any thoughts of 'I do – to make money' start popping into your head, might it be fair to describe making money as an outcome rather than a reason or purpose?

The challenge with the easy 'what' then 'how' approach is that it doesn't inspire either the listener or, more importantly, the speaker. It's logical and our brains can make sense of the information but there's no joy or passion involved in describing *how* one spends one's life.

The reason for this? It's a cultural thing and it's also a habitual thing and it prevents us from reminding others and ourselves of *why* we do what we do. The old phrase 'culture eats strategy for breakfast' holds true here. In other words, no matter how exciting your plans and intentions, we still tend to follow what everyone else does. So in this example, if everyone else uses the 'what' and 'how' when discussing or describing their work, there is overwhelming evidence to suggest that we will do the same.

Going against the grain, or standing out when others fit in, is not hard to do from a practical perspective, but it's *really* hard to do if you are not focused and determined to run your own race. Our rationale, why we get out of bed in the morning, lies hidden from our consciousness, and therefore our emotions, from day-to-day. As a result, more often than not, we never allow ourselves the privilege of realising our purpose. The challenge with this in turn is that we can be either going through the motions daily, without connecting emotionally to what we do, or worse still, we can be wasting time doing something that means little or nothing to us, apart from the practical necessity of supporting ourselves and our families.

In all likelihood, this is what Henry Thoreau meant when he described the following: '*The mass of men lead lives of quiet desperation, and go to the grave with the song still in them.*'

The magic of Sinek's talk reverses the trend and focuses on the 'why' as the enabler – it lies at the emotional centre of our brain and controls decision making. This is hugely important for two reasons. Firstly, understanding our 'why' gives us the motivation, the desire to achieve our goals. Without a 'why', there is every chance that you will lack the commitment to follow through and achieve your aims. Secondly, understanding our 'why' allows us to communicate from a place of certainty and passion, which in turn engages others at an emotional level, which as we know controls the decision-making muscle!

Let's return to Peter's story and have a think about his 'why'.

As you may remember, with his wife's support Peter had made a decision to change his life. Happily, he stayed at his job while he put the pieces of the jigsaw in place, but the decision had been made and the emotional change in him was as different as night from day. With regards to becoming clear about his 'why', he adopted a process called 'go there first'. This is a simple yet highly effective way of manifesting great results, and it's all based upon the fact that your brain can't tell the difference between something vividly imagined and something real. As a result, he imagined that he was already achieving what he wanted to achieve as vividly as possible and then answered the questions below to find his 'why'.

So there is a simple yet thought-provoking exercise that you could try and it goes as follows:

Imagine as clearly and as vividly as you can that you are doing brilliantly with your career plans and all is going as it should. Ask yourself the following:

- What will I see, hear and feel when I am doing what I love and what I'm good at?

- What will I be helping others to do?

- And what will that help them to do?

- And what's important to me about this?

This process bypasses our autopilot day-to-day thinking and peels away the outer consciousness, rather like the hackneyed layers of an onion, until subconscious drivers are revealed.

From your written answers, you should have some great insights into what really matters to you about what you aspire to achieve: your 'why'. Or at least a 'working why' that you can focus on and tweak as you go forward. Make sure you write it down and put it somewhere visible as a daily reminder.

The third stage in the journey involves the **E**ngage – the actions needed to kick-start your 'how'.

Statistically, the stage where we need to turn theory into practice is the biggest stumbling block of all when people are looking to make changes. The difference between *loving* the idea of writing a book, for example, and actually *doing* it are as far apart as the earth is from the moon.

As mentioned above, there are different reasons for this: lack of focus, lack of a 'why', apathy, habits, or fear of failure being the main suspects, among others. There are also some who are raring to go, but don't know where to start and this lack of knowledge can be paralysing just by itself. As a result, try not to overthink this and take the first step by doing something, however small – whether it's a phone call, or registering a website, or writing a blog. Together with the first steps, take the extra insurance of telling people about it. Statistically, the more people you engage in your development, the more likely you are to succeed.

Make sure that you keep the momentum going by committing to five new actions towards your goal every day. This is absolutely fantastic advice because these steps will make sure you are 'on your way' and the temptation to back out is harder the further in you are – in other words, by taking progressive steps you are, in effect, committing yourself.

However, if you are one of the 'I want to take action, but I don't want to get it wrong' brigade, here is a little rigour that you can build into your planning process:

- *What needs to happen in order for me to achieve X?*

  For example:

  Main focus areas / Research the market / Research target audience / Set milestones, both words and time / Remember my 'why' / Start

- *What are the main areas to focus on to get there?*

  Positioning / Market / Target customers / Creating valuable content / Packaging products and services / Routes to market and strategy

- *What are the specific tasks that I need to do for each of these focus areas? By when?*

  Remember, don't overthink these first steps, just take them!

  Action……………… *By when*……………

  Action……………… *By when*……………

Action.................... By when..............

Action.................... By when............

Action...................... By when..............

As far as Peter's story goes, his journey continued with the engage steps and was hugely helpful in establishing some real physical change, as opposed to the creative mental processes he had gone through thus far. Whilst these are straightforward in design, they are inevitably of enormous practical use because they gave him a structure to his plans.

Thus far, you have made a definite decision and really gained some clarity about why you are looking to make changes to your career. In addition, you have taken your first huge steps towards your goal.

The fourth thing to make sure of is to monitor, or **A**djust.

Confucius said: *'When it is obvious that the goals cannot be reached, don't adjust the goals, adjust the action steps.'*

Confucius is quite right in that what we tend to do when faced with challenges to our plans is to change the plans not the strategy. Why? Because it's easier.

As the saying goes: *'If you do what you've always done, you'll get what you've always got'* – in other words, you can't just blindly continue if the results aren't working, nor should you panic and change the goal. Things that you try won't always work because that's life, but if you are vigilant and make sure that you can judge how effective your strategy is, you remain proactively in control rather than reactively being controlled.

Instead, the solution is actually very simple. If you want a success formula that is bulletproof, you have to measure your progress to make sure that what you are doing is working, and if it isn't, you have to change your approach, or **A**djust. This is a simple process of regular monitoring, to see how well each of your concepts is being received.

But remember, change the approach *not* the goal!

Over the course of the next nine months, Peter was putting his plans into action. Naturally, things didn't always go as planned. He went, to a certain extent, through the 'school of hard knocks', but, sure of his goal, his 'why' and his action steps, he was enjoying the learning curve.

His actual goal was to become a professional performance coach for individuals and businesses, people development being his 'why', and as a result, he had engaged in a coaching diploma, together with accreditation in Neuro Linguistic Programming (NLP). Part of his accreditation was accruing lots of hours of *pro bono* coaching that he needed to monitor and several of these sessions were 'observed' as part of his course. Together with this, he was holding down a full-time job and was also constructing a website, scheduled to go live as soon as he qualified. You can be sure that there were a few bumps in the road as a result. However, he made sure that he did a weekly review to see which elements of his plan were on track and which needed a little more attention. For example, the easiest thing for him to do when a technical side of his website didn't work as he wanted would have been to either leave that element out altogether or procrastinate because he was a bit 'stuck'. But this of course would have been tantamount to changing the goal not the approach.

Being mindful of this was the difference that kept him on track; as a result, he would change his approach each time rather than burying his head in the sand. Not always easy to do, but as he later revealed, the more you practise something, the easier it becomes.

There's one more brilliant strategy that is also simple yet rigorous in the extreme and that's to **M**odel best practice. It stands to reason that, somewhere out there in your sphere, or at least within the sphere of people you know, there is someone who is doing what you want to do – better than you currently are.

Is that fair?

The question one might therefore ask is this: Success leaves clues. So what stops you from going to that person and asking for some pointers to how they do it?

The answers revolve around the following:

- Ego – we don't want to look or feel inferior to others

- Fear – we don't want people to refuse to help

- Lack of awareness – we just haven't thought about asking others who are doing what we aspire to do better because we are conditioned not to

The challenge here is that none of these reasons for not asking for advice make sense! As long as you ask with genuine interest and humility, the chances of our looking stupid or inferior when asking for advice is laughable. The same applies with our chances of others refusing to offer advice. It all depends upon the way we put it.

Modelling best practice represents a brilliant shortcut to achieving the results you want. In short, this is all about copying the precise strategies of those who are succeeding at what you want in order to achieve precisely identical results. For example, if you have ever copied a recipe from a cookbook, you have modelled best practice.

Why do it?

Competitive advantage. For the very good reason that you need to speed up your success in a world of stiff competition, where 'if you snooze, you lose'. The secret lies in firstly identifying who that person is. This is normally quite a simple process. If you can't think of an individual that you know personally who is achieving the results you want, more often than not someone in your circle of influence will.

Secondly, you need to find out what their secrets are. Whilst this may seem a simple task, might it be fair to suggest that if you ask someone who is good at something how they do it, they tend to reply, 'I don't know – I just do it'? As a result, the technique involves asking your respondent some questions that will make it easy for them to give you the information you need. For example, instead of 'How do you do it?' you might think of asking questions such as 'How do you prepare for X?' or 'What did you find most useful when you were learning about Y?' or 'What books have you read?' and so on.

The better the question, the better quality the answer.

Then lastly, all you need to do is to be prepared to try their strategies on for size. So go and find that model of excellence and find out some short cuts to great results. Just remember, if you copy precise strategies, you will get identical results.

This last step was one of the most important elements in the process for Peter. Because he was a novice in a new world, there were models of excellence everywhere he looked, from the organisers of his coaching diploma, to the networking group he joined for new entrepreneurs. In addition, for the technical side, he found models of IT excellence online – a great revelation this, to realise that he didn't actually have to know these people; as long as he could speak to them, even virtually, he had expertise to copy at the touch of a button.

The result? Peter is now a fully-fledged coach and mentor to both individuals and organisations, with a flourishing business and as much free time as he wants to devote to the really important things in his life. In fact, one of the mantras he lives by is the phrase 'Dream BIG!'

What you will gain by using the tools and techniques in this book

There are two main outcomes from reading this book: awareness and skills.

Awareness

The first aim of this book is to raise some awareness within you of what you are passionate about, and secondly, what you are really good at. The final aim is to raise some awareness within you of how you can package these passions and skills into easy-to-follow steps to solve challenges that others face in your field.

Skills

The outcome here is to learn an end-to-end solution for packaging your knowledge into content that is easy to teach, learn and understand, to grow a customer base and to engage and inspire *any* audience.

Here's a very quick insight into what you will learn:

- **Stand out**
  Most people have a deep and visceral fear of public speaking, so by definition, you become highly visible if you choose to put yourself through the process and skills that put you in the limelight

- **It's a numbers game**
  Why promote your products and services to a few when you can inspire many at the same time?

- **Position yourself** as a credible subject–matter expert through the art of the story

- **Build the most relevant structure** for your speeches and presentations, depending on the subject, the audience and the time you have

- **Learn framework techniques** that will make sure you never run out of things to say

- Access the **decision-making** part of your audience's brain

- **Understand and use the techniques for overcoming nerves** and taking to the stage with confidence and yes, enjoyment!

- **Create speeches** and presentations that ensure your audience gets value, has fun and most importantly, takes action at the end

- **Use focus to grab the audience's attention** and create hunger for your topic

- Learn and practise the skills of **charisma and credibility**

Why is public speaking the answer? In a poll conducted several years ago, it was discovered that mankind's greatest fear was... public speaking!

To give you an idea of how scary people find public speaking, death came third! (If you're interested, spiders came second!)

This raises several very important points:

By definition, you are highly visible if you choose to put yourself through public speaking as a profession. You become an outlier. It therefore follows that whilst public speaking may seem high risk to nine out of ten people, it is also high reward. In addition, it's a numbers game – public speaking is a great opportunity to stand out in front of lots of people at once.

Not only are you more visible, you also become respected by others. The concept of public speaking raises very visceral emotions in others, which is what you want. Here is a quote for you, from a debated source:

*'People may not remember what you said, but they will always remember how you made them **feel**.'*

People buy in emotionally. As a result, if you are great at public speaking, you will be in a far better position to influence the hearts of your audience (real) as well as their minds (right).

Your self-esteem rises. If you type into Google 'quotes around self-esteem', you will notice that there is a trend that soon establishes itself. Firstly, that self-esteem isn't governed by what other people think, and secondly, that self-esteem is experiential. Unless you take the leap of faith, you will never know what you are capable of. My master classes are all about practice in a safe environment. When you have tried it on for size, with constructive feedback from my pool of experts, you will find that you will surprise yourself with the feedback you receive. Think of the power of looking back and saying to yourself 'I've actually *done* that!'

The halo effect kicks in. It is a much documented fact that people who are seen to shine in one area of their life are perceived by others to have other areas of expertise as well. In other words, if you are seen to 'wow' people with your ability to stand and talk passionately about a subject, it stands to reason that people will see you as highly credible and therefore assume that you are highly credible in other areas of your life as well.

You are outside the comfort zone, which means you grow. In a recent survey, 100 top performers from the fields of sport and the military were asked to complete a series of questions around resilience. Two sets of questions were asked:

1. Firstly, they were asked what emotions they felt before the event in question, whether it be sporting (a race, for example) or military (a reconnaissance patrol in a battle zone).

2. Secondly, they were asked what their coping strategies were during the event itself.

These two sets of data compiled from these elite performers have now been calibrated, to the extent that individuals can now measure their own levels of resilience against world-class performance. But here's the thing: every single member of our elite poll stated categorically that they would prefer to be outside their comfort zone. They stated that, amongst other things, 'living on the edge' allows you to explore what you are capable of.

You influence the world around you. Look for the stories in your life – they are going on around you all the time. Remember, great stories happen to us all and are therefore the property of us all. They are happening to you and those with whom you interact every day. It's just a matter of switching off your autopilot and opening your eyes and ears.

Summary

Dare to **D R E A M:**

- Make a **D**ecision to change your life to the way you want it

- Find your 'why' or **R**ationale

- **E**ngage your gears and take action

- Be vigilant and **A**djust your strategy if necessary

- Lastly find a **M**odel of excellence and create a shortcut to the results you want

In addition, remember that there is no quicker or better way of building trust, likeability and credibility than through charismatic public speaking skills.

Brilliant face-to-face communication can be taught, charisma can be taught, influence can be taught, confidence can be taught. You don't have to have a natural talent for it, it can also be taught – and fast!

Public speaking is the most effective way of influencing large numbers of people at once. And if they know why they're there, they are already 'warm' prospects.

There is no better way to create new leads and to promote your business, because unlike group emails and even webinars, the face-to-face interaction builds both trust and lack of ambiguity.

There is no faster way of creating competitive advantage over your rivals than by learning the art of charisma, confidence and communication.

CHAPTER 2:
THE MINDSET

'Low self-confidence isn't a life sentence.'

Barrie Davenport

In this chapter we will be discussing the critical importance of mindset and the steps that constitute the difference that makes the difference:

– The S U C C E S S formula.

We have talked about the opportunity – this chapter is about you. In this chapter, we will look at the seven aspects of you as a communicator that define the difference between massive impact… and not.

The S U C C E S S formula:

Self-awareness

The ability to raise awareness of your habitual behaviours and to understand whether they are helping you or holding you back. Furthermore, the ability to highlight what you do when you are performing at your best.

Understanding

Developing deeper distinctions and understanding both from experimentation and by learning from your mistakes.

Craving

Playing to your passions and enjoying the hunger for your chosen topic.

Contribution

Realising the human need to make a difference to others as an enabler, helping people to unlock their potential.

Endeavour

The irresistible power of persistence.

Strategy

The strategy of success – bringing self-awareness to life in a simple yet painless self-development tool.

Self-belief is broken into three components:

1. An understanding of how beliefs work.

2. The ability to choose beliefs about yourself that will help you rather than hold you back; that help you to take action rather than avoiding situations.

3. The ability to see the positive in every situation, leaving you in a resourceful state every time.

These are the critical seven mindset disciplines that, if you follow them *consistently*, will create the following outcomes:

- You as an authority and an evangelistic communicator around your chosen subject and area of expertise

- You as a must-see for anyone wanting to improve their skills and boost their sales in your area of expertise

- You as a confident, happy and enthusiastic business person who relishes the prospect of developing others, celebrating success and learning from your mistakes

- You representing your best days consistently

In short, you as the inspiring professional that you always wanted to be.

If you feel that you only match these aspirational statements sporadically, here are each of the disciplines in a little more detail.

Self-awareness

Focus increases awareness – Awareness increases understanding

Understanding increases control – Control increases performance

Self-awareness is the cornerstone of learning, the eradicator of bad habits and the key to raising your skills and effectiveness to a world-class level.

Whenever people are asked how self-aware they feel themselves to be, the normal responses vary between 'moderately' and 'very'. Statistics differ with these convictions and the main consensus is that, whilst a desirable quality, being self-aware is actually very hard to achieve.

Again, if people are asked, 'How do you become self-aware?' the responses seem to be neither encouraging nor convincing. It's difficult; everyone knows we should have it, but it's hard to do, so with regards to finding self-awareness, we know that it's a good thing, but I think just a little understanding around what steps we need to take in order to raise our awareness of our habits – both good and bad – is probably a very good place to start.

In the last 15 years, the fields of Mindfulness and Emotional Intelligence have made strides in the right direction and there are various theories and approaches to achieving a heightened sense of self-awareness, but the best approach is actually very straightforward.

Human beings are creatures of habit. We are conditioned at an early age to follow what everyone else does. 'Stand up', 'sit down', 'brush your teeth', 'go to bed', 'eat your greens', 'do your homework' and so on. Therefore, as we grow up, we become conditioned to habitual behaviour, just as society dictates and our role models have done before us. Neuroscience tells us that there is part of the brain which responds to habitual process as well, which goes back to our primeval routes, where doing things consistently meant that we stayed alive rather than being eaten.

Of course, our habits aren't necessarily a bad thing; being a creature of habit is potentially good, so long as your habits are good! The challenge is that whilst many of our habits as adults in a modern world are helpful, we also have bad habits, which again because they are habitual, it's very difficult to become aware of what they are.

You may be asking the question, 'What does this have to do with the goals laid out in this book? Public speaking for example?'

Better communication being one of the main aims of this book, you need to understand that the first and most crucial thing to do is to become aware of what your habits are, both good and bad, so that you can build on the good habits and look to break the bad ones. The challenge is that without this sense check, you are in danger of never improving, however hard you work. Bearing this in mind, understanding how self-awareness can be mastered is essential.

Perhaps the simplest concept, and yet the most insightful, is a methodology that is applicable to any skill or process that you wish to improve and ultimately become expert in. It has several labels but is perhaps best known as the Four Steps to Learning, originally conceived by Gordon Training International back in the 70s. As the title implies, there are four very clear steps that you will have climbed if you've learned any process in your life. Each step has a different level of awareness and emotional connection.

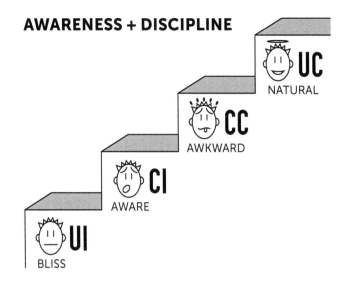

The journey starts, as with any climb, at the bottom, with step number one, which is **Unconscious Incompetence** – in other words, you don't know that you don't know. The emotional connection with this first step is carefree because you don't know that you don't know. Perhaps the best phrase that sums up the emotional connection with this first step is the adage 'ignorance is bliss'.

Unconscious incompetence is very easy.

Probably the most consistently told story with regards to the four steps is the analogy of learning to drive a car.

Imagine, if you will, an early memory of life, sitting astride a parent's knee, aged about five, with a toy steering wheel in your hands, having a whale of a time and squeaking, 'I'm driving.' Of course, you weren't aware that you didn't know how to drive, so you were therefore unconsciously incompetent.

That's the first step, but we need to keep moving. As we step up to step two, this is **Conscious Incompetence**.

You try something new and you realise that you don't know how to do it. We have gone from unconscious incompetence to conscious incompetence and, all of a sudden, there is a very big difference: your awareness has changed and you realise that you do not know how to do something. Not surprisingly, this can be very difficult to handle emotionally.

Picture again the scene where you then took a step up to the second step, or conscious incompetence, and you had your first driving lesson. That well-remembered feeling of nervousness when you lowered yourself into the driving seat for the first time, you looked down and you remember saying to yourself, with some dismay, 'Three pedals, two feet – there's a design fault here.' You sure as heck knew that you didn't know how to drive. It's the second step and, as mentioned, it's emotionally painful.

This applies to any new skill we either wish or need to learn. So you are emotionally challenged as you look to get to grips with whatever this new technique may be – it's never nice to know one's own lack of skill in a certain area of life.

You are now at the hardest part of the journey, both technically as you learn new skills as well as emotionally, because you keep getting it wrong in your efforts to improve. Finally, however, after much hard work, you reach step three, which is **Conscious Competence**: you can do it, after much trial and error, but you have to think about it really hard. Emotionally, you have survived the worst, although the new process is taxing; you have to focus and concentrate to get the job done, which can be awkward and demands resilience.

If we stay with our example of you learning to drive, you may remember turning the steering wheel by feeding it through your hands, which isn't the natural process for an accustomed driver. There was also a process that everyone gets taught, which is a sequence: do you remember 'mirror, signal, manoeuvre'? Now again, if you remember how awkward that was – you looked in the mirror, you indicated and then you 'fed' the wheel – it wasn't exactly the most natural of processes. It was a learnt competence, but it was quite awkward at the same time.

After a great deal of practice (according to various different studies, approximately 66 days' worth) you finally arrive at step number four, which is **Unconscious Competence**. You've made it. You're doing something that you know how to do so well that it has become habitual; you don't think about it anymore and it's easy. Emotionally, it stands to reason that anything that you have practised to the extent that you no longer think about it is natural and stress-free.

If you think once more about the analogy of driving a car, you don't think about the process of changing gear or using the clutch and accelerator when you're driving, especially those who drive automatic cars, which seems to be the majority of cars these days. You don't think about the process of brake and accelerator and engaging drive, you just do it.

Of course you're watching the road, but the mechanics of driving are ingrained and embedded in your habitual brain. So as a result, you have now reached the fourth step, unconscious competence, where you are habitual. The autopilot is on and we have formed a habit that is helping us.

The challenge comes where you are habitually able to do something, but you've become so used to it that it's easy to take shortcuts and to get into bad habits.

The laws of nature tell us that if we don't grow, we die. It's really important to realise how the four steps to learning work, if you are going to employ a rigorous approach to improving your expertise rather than standing still – which inevitably means decline.

So if we continue with the analogy of driving a car, imagine that you know that it is bad practice and a bad habit to hold the telephone to your ear while you're driving. We all know that this is a bad habit but it doesn't stop us doing it. However, an article in a national newspaper actually reported seeing someone driving down the road recently with a mobile phone in one hand and a cappuccino in the other. It does start to beg the question what he was driving the car with!

The answer to remaining aware of our strengths and to eradicating bad habits, then, is to switch off our autopilot and step off the top step of unconscious competence if we want to understand where our strengths and areas for improvement lie. In other words, we need to understand how to maintain and improve our performance in any area of our lives because we are habitual in every area of our lives.

We are habitual with our relationships. We are habitual when we go shopping, we are habitual with the way we cook, the way we eat, the way we exercise, the way we relate to others, the way we communicate, the way we do odd jobs – all of this is habitual, it is ingrained.

Now most of our habits of autopilot behaviour will be good. Some of them, however, as with the analogy about driving with a mobile phone and a cappuccino, will have slipped into bad habits, as a result of taking an easy route to achieve competence.

So when we come to communication, it is the same as any other part of our lives. We need to switch off the autopilot, step off our unconsciously competent step and come down two steps, to conscious incompetence again. So we become aware of what it is we are doing, both good and bad. Now we're actually becoming aware of our good habits. It's immensely powerful because we can then work on improving those skills. The other benefit is that once we are aware of what our bad habits are, we can start to focus on how we can change those bad habits and turn them into good ones.

Best practice case study – 'Success Leaves Clues'

I once mentored someone who had lots of corporate experience and wanted to move from his desk to his feet on a stage. The scenario was certainly helpful for him in that we were paired together to deliver a long-lasting global sequence of seminars to various branches of a corporate bank, the duration of which, with a few short breaks, was going to last six months. In other words, he was going to get a great deal of practice!

We started in Tokyo and I got a really good look at his style on stage. In awareness terms, he was on step two (conscious incompetence) with regards to his subject matter knowledge and communicated with the audience from step four (unconscious competence habit), where he displayed lots of natural qualities that worked and some that didn't, as one would expect. Seeing the future possibilities of becoming a proficient public speaker, he immediately looked to get to grips with a deeper understanding of the material. We had lots of time on our hands as we moved through the Asia Pacific region and I remember our long-haul night flights and endless conversations with him around designing compelling content, tips for engaging an audience and general communication skills, as our fellow passengers snored around us.

So the first thing that resonated with me about the frankly impressive journey that this individual took was his insatiable appetite for learning deeper distinctions about the material that he was delivering.

But it wasn't just the appetite, it was also the manner in which he learned that was clearly making a huge difference both to his improvement and the value that his audience received as a result. He would first talk through his understanding of the material in question. He would ask for my thoughts and then bombard me with question after question, writing down the answers. He would then read through them over and over again and would insist on my immediate feedback after each subsequent delivery on stage, both of deeper distinctions around the material as well as specific feedback on his fast developing skills in communication.

This feedback would comprise three elements and involved conversation and writing:

1. What worked well.

2. What didn't work as well as expected but provided insight.

3. What to change for next time.

The final – and most noticeable – tactic he used was a fearless approach of experimenting 'live'. Whilst endless conversations went on prior to the delivery of his content, he quickly got into the habit of trying a new technique, or telling a new story without extensive rehearsal, thereby giving him very testing high-stakes environments in which to practise. There was no safety net and whilst some experiments worked better than others, he found that there was no time where he would even be close to 'dying on his feet'.

We called this battle-hardening process 'The Teflon Technique' – where he was developing huge resilience in pretty extreme heat, adopting a 'non-stick attitude' where nothing could distract or dishearten him. It was a privilege to sit at the back of the hall and watch him experiment, not only with the content or technique in question, but also with his emotional state under pressure and also that of his audience.

It was only through testing himself under severe pressure that he grew to understand his own coping strategies and also understand what would or would not work, with large, often cynical and highly analytical audiences of senior investment bankers.

After the first couple of months, he was generally at the high end of conscious competence with the content of his speeches, still very much aware of the process and yet many of his communication techniques had moved even higher, to unconscious competence, where he was operating technically from his unconscious mind. He had moved up the stepladder, using a set of extremely potent tools.

What made this possible?

- He was willing to 'fail'

- He worked very hard at understanding deeper distinctions

- He had no ego at all and was willing to admit his shortcomings

- He had lots of courage and put himself purposefully under enormous pressure to understand himself better and also to understand what worked and what didn't

- He planned his way to **SUCCESS:**

  Self-awareness

  Understanding (seeking to get deeper and deeper distinctions)

  Craving (hunger to learn, practise, improve)

  Contribution (a desire to be of value)

  Endeavour (writing, asking questions, and practise, practise, practise)

  Strategy (rejoice, reframe, refine)

  Self-belief (trust of ability)

An understanding of the four steps to learning and active application of switching off our autopilot will raise awareness of what we are doing well, any bad habits we have crept into, and will also help us to focus on improving our skills in any area.

No one would have an easy conscience when recommending anyone to use public speaking as a means of growing their reputation, and their business accordingly, without being clear that the word 'journey' is well advised. Anyone who feels that they have mastered the art is dreaming. It's a learning process that never ends. The best advice we can take, then, is to build our level of self-awareness in the context of speaking in public and this will serve us well.

Don't forget too, that we are currently experiencing the fastest growing boom of the internet age, with new platforms popping up like rashes. If Facebook were a country, it would have the biggest population in the world at 1.39 billion users and YouTube has over a billion visits a month as well. If you are serious about building your public speaking brand, remember that an awareness, and use of the internet's social media resources, will be a key differentiator in your future success. As well as this, your knowledge of what's new and what you can use to be at the forefront in marketing both yourself and your brand will give you competitive advantage, but you have to keep your finger on the pulse and remain aware of what's happening because otherwise you will be left behind. Without self-awareness, you are flying blind.

Understanding

A good question to ask yourself is, 'What else can I learn about this? What books are there on this topic? What downloads/case studies/ blogs can I find out about?' There is always more to find out about a subject which will give you added insights on top of those that you have already learnt. Don't be complacent – always look for deeper understanding. You can't go far wrong if you keep asking yourself the question, 'What else can I do?'

And as well as this, you are looking to become even more knowledgeable in your chosen area. One of the key ingredients of credibility lies in subject matter expertise. You will only do yourself good by setting yourself targets to find out new distinctions each week. Give yourself a clear goal to do this.

A power base of robust skills-based knowledge is the answer. Whilst supplementary reading is hugely beneficial and invaluable in many ways, reading alone will not get it done. It's a great start, but experience tells us that nothing will build the knowledge skills and confidence faster than practice. If you can find a way to turn theory into practice on a regular basis, you will be hard-wiring your new-found skills in the best way possible. This is because you will understand not only the techniques but also how your delivery of them lands. The more you practise, the quicker your expertise will grow.

This having been said, practice of course is not always realistically possible, as there may not be a willing audience to hand every time you want to work through some new ideas. It's also important to remember that the goodwill of friends and family can be abused!

Craving

Perhaps the most important thing to have is a passion for your subject – a hunger for both knowledge *and* improved skills. The word is used advisedly. There are two ways of describing this: one is (on the whole) pleasurable and the other disaster. However, both examples reflect the depth of emotion and investment of focus and attention that you will need in order to follow through on your plans.

Perhaps the most engaging and pleasurable analogy to sum up the craving element is to remember – if you have ever been lucky enough to experience this – falling in love (so long as the other person ended up feeling the same). Your whole world takes on a new meaning. Everything is channelled through the filter of your new and burgeoning autofocus on someone else. Your everyday commute suddenly becomes an opportunity for a weekend walk with your beloved to explore the area you have passed without thinking every day for so long. The book you may be reading is now channelled through not only your own perception but also the wondering of whether this new person in your life would feel the same way as you do about the book in question. When you eat, you wonder if the other person in question might also enjoy the food you are eating.

Enough of the analogy, but the importance of setting your RAS in line with your goal is clear. In a way, we are talking about a healthy form of addiction, of obsession. This is a self-taught, self-regulated process, which should be fed and nurtured on a daily basis. If you can filter your experiences through the lens of an obsession with learning and communication, you can be assured that your life will change. As mentioned in Chapter 1, the reason why it's so important to have a passion for what you do on a daily basis is that without the hunger, you will wilt. It's a law of nature.

Contribution

What was consistently impressive about this individual was his desire to 'be of value' to his audience. Whilst he felt totally passionate about his subject and was hungry to learn as much as possible, the message that was received from his work, and the reason that it was so successful, was that the audiences that he addressed could be in no doubt that he cared deeply about their comprehension, their curiosity and their eventual takeaways. He would leave no stone unturned in his efforts to give value to every member of every audience he worked with. He also made a point of going above and beyond what might have been expected from a speaker, in that he would devote time after his sessions to answering questions and giving advice to all comers.

There are many motivators that guide us as humans, the most simplified of which are the desire to gain pleasure and the desire to avoid pain, which can be seen as overarching impulses. But lying underneath these are some real needs that we all feel as humans, one of which is the need to contribute.

And moreover, there is much statistical data which suggests the following:

Contributing to others makes us feel happy

Over and above our instinctive understanding that we get a good feeling from helping others, neuroscience research has identified that receptors in our brain release endorphins when we contribute to others' welfare.

Contributing to others is good for our health

Amazingly, researchers have found consistent supporting data that if you give selflessly to others your life expectancy increases, and the likelihood of your contracting life-threatening diseases decreases.

Contributing to others promotes gratitude

I'm not saying that giving to others means they'll be grateful to *you*. What I mean is that 'an attitude of gratitude' encourages individuals to raise awareness and open their eyes to the good things in their lives, as opposed to focusing on the less positive aspects encouraged by the conditioning of modern society.

Contributing to others is infectious

Jack Nicholson's character in *As Good As It Gets* sums this up beautifully. When struck by the openness and generosity of spirit displayed by Helen Hunt's character, Carol the waitress, he tells her, 'You make me want to be a better man.'

When you help others for no personal gain, it inspires.

Endeavour

There's a quote that always sticks in the mind by Benjamin Franklin, which goes as follows: *'Energy and persistence conquer all things.'* There is endless precedent supporting the value of hard work, from Thomas Edison and his reputed 10,000 attempts to perfect the light bulb, to Van Gogh who painted 800 works in his life and sold just one, to modern giants such as JK Rowling who, richer than the Queen, wrote her first Harry Potter book on a manual typewriter as a struggling single parent and had her manuscript rejected 12 times. Imagine if she'd given up after 11.

Endeavour can be engrained through discipline. We all know that hard work is a good thing, the trick is to make it a habit. In the same way that, as children, the last thing we wanted to do at bedtime was to brush our teeth, so we wouldn't dream of not brushing our teeth twice a day as adults. So somewhere in there, late childhood or adolescence, we have a) realised the value of the toothbrush (seeing the big picture – we won't be attractive to anyone if our teeth fall out!) and b) applied some self-discipline as a result.

The secret seems to be then, that in order for you to endeavour, you need first to see the value of doing so and to raise some awareness as to the importance to you of achieving the goal you are attempting to reach. In the story mentioned above, our friend embraced hard work. By going above and beyond the reasonable limits expected of an average public speaking professional, he was proving to himself on a daily basis that, in his words, 'if it's worthwhile, it's got to hurt.'

You have to practise

Did you ever see the original series of *Karate Kid* movies in the 1980s? You may remember the bullied teenager, Daniel LaRusso, who has moved from New Jersey to California and is having trouble fitting in, to the extent that his new love interest is the ex-girlfriend of the school tough and karate expert Johnny. Life is literally the school of hard knocks until the caretaker of his apartment block, Mr Miyagi, who happens to be a karate expert, rescues him from one particularly nasty beating. Miyagi agrees to train Daniel in the art of karate, more as a life discipline than as a means of taking revenge and, in the process, Daniel learns the discipline of practice as much as anything else. If you have seen it, you will remember that Daniel has many tasks to perform that he sees as slave labour: waxing cars, sanding floors, painting fences and even Miyagi's house. But unbeknownst to him, the wily old master has been engraining the karate moves into his student through these chores with huge amounts of repetition and practice, so that his skill is growing even though he does not realise it.

Now whilst this movie didn't win best acting Oscars, it is nonetheless a cult movie possibly because of its underlying message – a particularly effective example of the saying 'practice pays'.

Everything is a willingness to practise – and then practise, practise and practise some more – until your skills are hard-wired and improved to the level where you have instant credibility in that area and are recognised as a go-to specialist. There is sadly no silver bullet, but do the work and focus on your goal; the reason why you are working so hard and the chore can become a real pleasure.

Strategy

'He believed in himself, believed in his quixotic ambition, letting the failures of the previous day disappear as each new day dawned. Yesterday was not today. The past did not predict the future if he could learn from his mistakes.' Daniel Wallace

According to many, it was Einstein whose definition of insanity was 'doing the same thing over and over again and expecting a different result'. In the same way that an insect will bash its head against a pane of glass until it succumbs to concussion, we as humans are habitual animals who live our lives on autopilot. In our daily routines, we are so conditioned that we don't focus upon whether our daily habits – in anything – are helping, or holding us back.

Without a strategy or a benchmark for improvement, it is impossible for us to have any idea of our progress towards any goal.

Enter our friend's 'success ritual'. It was very simple. The idea was to receive regular feedback about his performance, split into three very simple areas:

1. What did I do well, or was received well? **(rejoice)**

2. What didn't work as well as I hoped but provided a good learning experience? **(reframe)**

3. And therefore, what do I need to do differently next time? **(refine)**

The advantages to following a simple strategy of self-improvement are several.

Let's look at the **rejoice** part first.

The value of reflecting upon daily successes in a given area of focus is huge because we don't normally celebrate success in our lives. Think of our society. As children, we are conditioned to rely on others; we have a dependency mindset created by others telling us what to do and when to do it. 'Sit down, stand up, eat your greens, brush your teeth' – and so on. It's not surprising that we develop habitual patterns, designed and developed by others, that we simply don't question because these things have become part of our daily routine. Now we're not saying that the habits formed are necessarily bad – they're not. In fact most of them are good, resourceful behaviour patterns that serve us well.

The challenge with cultural conditioning, however, is that whilst it serves to shield us from inconsistency, it also prevents us from 'tweaking' habits that we may have outgrown, or from improving the efficiency of what we have learnt long ago and forgotten the ingredients of.

The other thing to consider is how we continue to be conditioned as we go through our lives. It's a well-documented fact that clever marketeers 'own' part of our brains by drip-feeding their images and slogans into our lives. This is how brand loyalty is positioned into our brains. Imagine you are browsing supermarket shelves and looking for a breakfast cereal, for example. Statistics show that as we compare an 'own brand' created by the supermarket next to the well-known and well-advertised market leader, more often than not a little voice goes off in our head, saying something like 'I think you'll find that brand X is the way to go.'

Why? Because we've been drip-fed brand X, either consciously or subconsciously, on banner advertising, TV and radio slogans, billboards, celebrity endorsement etc. until that particular brand is synonymously linked to the cereal itself. We may think that we control our decision making, but there is a lot of automatic response built into our daily lives as a result of advertising that we are simply not aware of.

Moreover, we are not conditioned to look at the optimistic side of life either. If you are a parent, I would ask you to consider the scenario when your child returns home with a report card from school. As a conditioned response, do you focus more attention on the A's and the B's, or the D's and the E's? As a society, we are conditioned not to look at the positive but at the negative side to life. In a similar way to the school report, our minds are geared towards the negative by our daily dose of the news, whether in newspaper form or on TV.

Bad news sells – period.

Unfortunately, whilst bad news sells, we suffer as a result because our conditioned life response is to focus upon the negative – upon what *isn't* working, rather than what is. This is the reason why the **rejoice** part of the equation is in place. This is to get you to switch off your autopilot conditioned response of focusing on what's wrong or broken and instead getting into the habit of looking for the positive in every situation. In practical terms, this means a daily reminder to remember that you are succeeding every day; the challenge is that you are too busy focusing on what isn't working, rather than on what is.

Picture the scene: You arrive at work at, say, 8.30am. You greet your colleagues as usual and start your daily routine. All progresses well throughout the morning and your output is satisfactory, as is your administrative workload and your meetings and phone calls.

Lunch is also productive – you are working on a project and have a sandwich at your desk. All is in order as you reflect upon what has been done so far today and what you still have to do before clocking off at 5.30pm.

Suddenly, all hell breaks loose. There is a major problem. Your firm's biggest client, with whom you have the original relationship, calls you to say that he is 'disgusted' with the service provided by your firm. He has very poor feedback about the account management skills of your colleagues, with the implication that you are to blame as the main project contact. Moreover, the client informs you that the timing is coincidental with the annual vendor review at your client's headquarters and that he feels it only fair to warn you that he will be representing you and your company in a very poor light as a result of his recent experience.

You know that your arch-rivals and biggest overall competitor have been courting this client for some time in the hope of just such a situation. Your fears are not exactly helped by the pointed way in which your client mentions as a final flourish to the phone call that he has been asked to a top sporting event as their guest the following week.

How would you be feeling? Panic, right? Suddenly, everything is 'on the line' – you see your professional life flashing before your eyes. But being the consummate professional that you are, you think and act fast and with decision. You contact everyone involved and call an emergency meeting before deciding upon an action plan, which you are required to go and present to the board.

Somehow, you get through the day; you have been to see the client personally and have made certain guarantees that are above and beyond the call of duty and you feel that the situation has been rescued from the jaws of disaster – just.

You arrive home late, stagger through the front door and you hear your 'other half' ask, 'How was your day?' Might it be fair enough to suggest that your response would be less than cheery? Something along the lines of 'nightmare' or 'awful', right?

Whilst an exaggerated scenario, what's the moral to this story?

We all find it easy to look at the disasters in our day – the month at the end of the money/the toast falling jam-side down/the bad weather/the queues/other people not fitting our ideal – because that's what everyone else does and we have been taught/conditioned to look at the negative all our lives. But even in this extreme example mentioned here, where everything was fine from 8.30am until 3pm, it is easy to forget that *good things happen every day.* The key is to acknowledge this, whatever else happens.

And what does recognition of daily achievement give us?

- A reminder that we are doing things right every day will give us confidence

- A reminder that we are doing things right every day will provide us with the means to measure our success

- A reminder that we are doing things right every day will enable us to fight the global culture of pessimism

So, that's the **rejoice** part. Even by itself, without the other two elements, it's a profound builder of 'self' (esteem, confidence and belief).

The second step in the improvement strategy is the **reframe.**

So what is reframing? According to Wikipedia, reframing is described as follows: *'a way of viewing and experiencing events, ideas, concepts and emotions to find more positive alternatives.'*

Why is reframing necessary? Very much in the same way as we are conditioned to look for the negative meaning in our experiences, so we are also conditioned by society to describe things that haven't succeeded as 'losing' or 'failure'.

No one actually likes to lose, or to fail; the challenge is that we do what everyone else does and we assign a pessimistic label to the things that we attempt and that don't work. Think about it: every company, large or small, has the same approach – any pitch, or campaign, or push for more sales, or change initiative that doesn't succeed is called... you guessed it, a failure.

The same applies to our individual attempts in life. Whatever we attempt without success is labelled a failure. 'What's wrong with that?' you might ask. 'The word is a recognised part of our everyday lexicon – it's not a swear word. Get over it.'

Agreed. The word 'failure' is a descriptive and easily understood word, which has its place when describing events that may have happened in the past, or in generalised speech not relating to personal endeavour. When casually used about corporate or individual behaviour, however, it is suggested that it has a powerful negative impact upon future attempts at success.

To explain: when you try something that doesn't work and your attempts are labelled by you and by others as a 'failure', this means pain. Look at the dictionary definition: *non-success, non-fulfilment, abortion, miscarriage, defeat, frustration, collapse.*

None of these are exactly encouraging. And this is precisely the point. There is no hope if you use the word 'failure'. It always has and it always will have painful associations. And the reason it is so dangerous is that if we attempt to succeed again and our efforts are in vain, what's it called again – by ourselves and by others? You guessed it: failure.

That's twice now that you have 'failed'. The pain is getting worse. If the danger area involves part of your job and you are compelled to attempt the challenge again and it doesn't work one more time, it just reinforces the negative impact of non-success. And this is where the real damage occurs. If we continue to attempt something that doesn't succeed and we label our attempts as failures time and again, what are we going to do eventually?

That's right – we're going to avoid doing it because it means pain.

And here's the thing: in extreme cases, where many attempts have been made and the pain level is high, we are even in danger of labelling ourselves in the same light, as 'a failure'.

Not good.

Failure avoidance is also success avoidance. You can't achieve anything without attempting to achieve. But if you are unwilling to attempt something because you are afraid of the pain of failing, how can you possibly succeed? Think of the analogy of a baby learning to walk. Does it succeed first time? Very rarely. There is lots of trial and error but it's unthinkable that the baby will give up when it doesn't succeed. At a primitive level, the baby knows that in order to improve it has got to 'fail' and keep doing it. As parents, we know that the baby will only learn to walk if it keeps trying. That's how it improves.

And as we look at our adult lives, isn't it true that the only way of improving is by making mistakes? It's hard to think of a single example where we are immediately proficient at a new skill. It's a law of nature, we can't run until we have learned to walk.

Success is only achieved through experience. Some would say – even many would say – that life is about the journey, not the destination. The journey is the suffering, the trial and error, the school of hard knocks and the knocks are what make us perfect. So what we have to do is to be able to thrive in that area of mistakes and mishaps, and in order for us to do that, we need to **reframe** the word 'failure', which will hard-wire a resourceful new habit of experimentation in an area that others will struggle in.

We have talked in some detail about the importance of switching off the autopilot and raising awareness of our habitual behaviour. So step 1 is to make a conscious decision to reframe and rename the word 'failure' to a more positive alternative.

Think about the massive difference here. Who likes to fail? No one. Who likes to learn? Everyone. So the idea here is to make a seemingly small change in mindset. If you see things that don't work as 'failures' or 'losses', you will not want to experiment, to persist. So the trick is to move from 'lose' to 'learn' and to make failure a thing of the past. All you need to do now is to either *rejoice* at your successes or to *reframe* your failures into 'learns' how to succeed the next time.

There is a final step in the ritual and that is the *refine* element. It is not enough to just reframe our 'failures' into 'learns', as this will only change our emotions and attitudes to our challenges, but not our outcomes. If we wish to improve our performance in a conscious and measured way, we need to employ learnt mindfulness, so that we can judge whether or not our attempts to succeed are working or not – and if not, to refine or tweak our approach until we find a solution that gives us the required outcome.

Moreover, this isn't a one-time refinement. In a changing environment, we need to be vigilant because our refinements which may well work today may be outgrown with tomorrow's changing landscape and tomorrow's outcomes.

Practical application

So how does this strategy actually pan out in practice?

1. Buy a journal.

2. Monitor your progress and remember that, like a game of golf, your ability will always be developing with your experience:

   • Remember firstly to be clear about your focus for development – or improvement area

   • Write your improvement area at the top of the page, with the words 'rejoice', then 'reframe' and lastly 'refine' at regular intervals down the left hand side

Make sure you devote ten minutes at least twice a week to writing down your findings: what's working well (rejoice), what's not (reframe), so what do I need to do differently next time (refine). Try to make these sessions part of your working hours, for the obvious reason that this will make your new habit easier to form with regularity. If you don't do this during work hours, other priorities in life will kick in.

Next, whenever you have a live practice – for example, if your improvement area is eye contact – you might take five minutes at some point after giving your speech to write down your findings. If you can get others' feedback as well, all the better; take the time to write down what you, and others if possible, see as the positive or plus points of the experience. Then, next to 'reframe', you need to write down what you (and others) felt could have been done better. And for each of these points, you need to write down what your 'refine' tasks are – in other words, what are you going to tweak for next time?

Focus Area: Gestures
Rome speech on 26/5

Rejoice:
- Itemising on Agenda first item, second item, third item
- Step forward, palms down to make main point
- Descriptive - East/West + senior v junior

Reframe:
- Missed a great opportunity to use an emphatic gesture at end
  ↳ Refine - More planning for end needed

Reframe:
- Didn't have time to rehearse
  ↳ Refine - Make rehearsal time a priority

Self-belief

The individual in my personal story followed all the steps mentioned above, but one thing underpinned his motivation to improve, learn and thrive and that was his unshakeable belief in himself.

Why is self-belief such an important part of promoting yourself and your business if you know your stuff already?

Build a powerful self-identity

Beliefs are the unseen, subconscious drivers of our lives. Essentially, a belief is a feeling of certainty – about anything at all. Our beliefs do not have to be based in fact, but they *do* have to be based in certainty.

Whenever you have an argument, it's all about beliefs: your feelings of certainty conflicting with someone else's. Whenever you make a statement or voice an opinion, your beliefs are at play: you are expressing feelings of certainty.

Just to be clear, we are not talking about our guiding values but more the inherent dialogue, both internal and external, that we have on a daily basis. Whenever you say, either to yourself or others, 'I can/I can't', 'It's possible/impossible', 'You're wrong, I'm right', 'I am/I am not', 'It is/it isn't' etc., you are expressing beliefs, your feelings of certainty.

Self-talk

When an audience is asked, 'Hands up if you speak to yourself', it will generally get about 60% of the room holding up their hands. The rest of the audience will be looking at the ceiling, literally asking themselves, 'Do I?' It's always a good moment.

We all talk to ourselves; it's a perfectly natural process and part of our thinking process. What we do not realise is that we spend much of our daily lives having an inner conversation. Most of us do this internally, but some people will also admit (privately, perhaps!) that they also speak to themselves out loud on occasion as well. The challenge can often be that what we are saying without realising it is perhaps not as helpful as we would like.

Picture the scene: You are about to step on to a stage to give a talk to a large audience – what's going through your head? Typically, you will have prepared well, but it's still a challenging situation because statistically people see this as more scary than dying! So, phrases like 'I can't wait for this to be over' or 'I'm terrified' tend to be the kind of thing that we say to ourselves.

Here's the thing: is this kind of self-talk helping us or hindering us? The answer is clear. And furthermore, it's also self-evident that what we say to ourselves tends to affect how we feel. If we go further down the track, how we feel affects our behaviour (what we say and what we do) and our behaviour affects our results. So in this light, what we say to ourselves is of huge importance.

We might say to ourselves on the one hand, 'I can do this' or, on the other hand, we might say, 'This is a nightmare.' We might say, 'I'm a natural communicator' or we might say, 'I'm quite shy.'

These are beliefs. And these two sets of beliefs drive completely different results, either positive or negative.

The question is why? An important thing to remember is this: what we feel to be true drives our feelings and emotions. Isn't that true? If you say to yourself, 'I can' it creates an emotion. If you say, 'I can't' it creates an emotion. Our feelings and emotions affect our behaviour – what we say and what we do. Our behaviour affects our performance and results.

So, in a nutshell, *our beliefs drive our performance and results.*

The next important point to make is that it's our brain's job to be 'right'. When we hold something to be true, our brain filters out any information that conflicts with our belief and only looks for information that will support it. For example, if you believe that you can just about get through your speech without making a fool of yourself, two things will happen.

Firstly, your belief in your lack of ability to achieve great results will not be helpful. After all, if you think you won't succeed, why bother trying, right? This belief will drive the chain reaction we talked about and you will not be in the best emotional state to deliver your speech.

Secondly, as you deliver your speech you will be looking not for enthusiastic response but for boredom, lack of focus, amusement (for the wrong reasons) etc. and ignoring any potentially positive responses.

Is it fair to suggest that the results you get are very unlikely to be as good as you might hope? Happily, the opposite is also true.

If you feel confident, your sense of belief will drive resourceful emotions and body language and you will be looking for the engaged members of the audience and ignoring everything else. In essence, you will be tapping into more potential. You have the expectation of a successful result, which will free up your confident, passionate self, which enjoys the limelight.

The result? You are far more likely to succeed because your beliefs have allowed your potential to shine through.

The challenge with limiting beliefs is that they are cyclical and scenarios play out as self-fulfilling prophesies. An estimated 98% of the beliefs you have on a daily basis will repeat themselves on a daily basis. You believe you won't succeed, which drives your less than positive results. This result then *reinforces* the original belief: I *knew* it wouldn't work.

So the key here is to get you into the position where your beliefs are resourceful and positive because then the chain reaction kicks in and the great results with it. Beliefs are either the secret for success or the recipe for disaster.

The path to success is, once again, all about awareness.

The key to great results as far as beliefs are concerned is the knowledge that *what we believe is a choice*. It may not feel like a choice, but nonetheless, what you believe can be conscious. You can choose beliefs that help you, or conversely you can choose beliefs that hold you back. The trick is to take a step back and think about the beliefs that you currently hold, helpful and unhelpful, and to consciously choose and reinforce the helpful ones and to discard the unhelpful ones consciously.

We know that beliefs are hugely important, but in order to start making informed choices that are congruent and realistic, we need to understand where they come from.

- From our environment and culture

- From our friends, family and colleagues

  (Think about the scenario where you are either sitting round a table with your family or in a bar or restaurant with friends – or an office with your colleagues. One of these talks about an experience they may have had and their beliefs about that experience. If you trust that person, is it not true that you take on their beliefs without necessarily challenging them?)

- From our role models

- From our experiences (and other people's experiences)

- From information sources (media, books etc.)

- From our imagination

All these various sources point to a random gathering of information. Why is this relevant?

According to statistics, we hear that we have approximately 60,000 thoughts a day, 98% of which will repeat themselves daily on a never ending spin cycle! This is of course wonderful news when we consider our helpful beliefs, that are being reproduced and therefore strengthening each and every day. It is less encouraging when we consider our limiting beliefs however.

There is encouraging news in the further statistic that approximately 1% of our beliefs are based in actual fact. The rest, as we have seen, come from generalisations, deletions, distortions, what we are told or have read.

Why is this great news?

It means simply that approximately 99% of our limiting beliefs are not actually based in fact and therefore can be challenged.

How do I change my limiting beliefs?

Thus far we have looked at what beliefs are, how beliefs work – i.e. how they drive our behaviour and our performance – and where beliefs come from. We know that what we believe drives either positive results or unhelpful ones based on whether they are empowering or limiting beliefs. So the key question has to be how do we get rid of our limiting beliefs?

There are three steps:

Step 1 – Raise awareness

The first thing to become aware of is what your limiting beliefs *are.* Remember, our beliefs tend to run the show subconsciously; we tend not to register what we are believing from moment to moment, but we have an emotional reaction to an event and our behaviour follows accordingly.

Have a think and make a list of any limiting beliefs that you have about:

- Your ability

- Your potential

- Your intelligence

- Your confidence

- Your knowledge

- Your credibility

- Your communication skills

- Your appearance

When you look at each of these in turn, you should be able to identify any niggling thoughts (and therefore beliefs) that you have.

A belief is similar to a tree, supported by roots that hold it up. The roots are references that support the belief. To keep the tree strong, it needs strong roots. For example, if you have a belief that 'I am a great public speaker' (tree), you will have several references to support this belief (roots), such as 'I got great feedback for my last speech', or 'I had 20 emails of congratulations after my last speech', or 'I've been asked to speak at my annual conference this year on the recommendation of my department'.

Unfortunately, exactly the same knock-on effect is in place for your unhelpful, or limiting, beliefs. For example, 'I'm not smart enough to handle difficult questions' (tree), with 'roots' such as 'I had no idea what to say when so-and-so asked that question', or 'I was completely tongue-tied last week at that meeting'.

The idea here is to leave the helpful or empowering beliefs alone and to cast doubt about any limiting ones you may have.

Step 2 – Challenge our unhelpful beliefs

We can shake the roots of our limiting beliefs by challenging them with questions.

Question 1 – Am I certain that this belief is true? (remember, 99% of the time you *can't* be certain!)

Question 2 – What difference would it make to my performance if I didn't have this belief?

Question 3 – Given that what I believe is a choice, what might be a more helpful belief to choose?

The key here is to remember that each question builds a case that successively weakens the belief.

The great thing about these questions is that they really do work – it's just a matter of remembering to use them rather than letting the daily cycle of your limiting beliefs run you.

Step 3 – Remind yourself of your greatness

It's one thing to challenge your limiting beliefs. That's a great start. But we can also use beliefs proactively to create an unstoppable powerful identity; to define a compelling future for ourselves based upon our qualities and our life experience.

I run two-day seminars on building bulletproof self-belief, where each individual gets the chance to really focus on their individual belief systems, but in the meantime, here's a slightly abridged explanation of how you can get your beliefs to work for you rather than against you.

As humans, we all have fears. There are six main ones:

1. Rejection

2. Failure

3. Loss

4. Embarrassment

5. Exposure

6. Conflict

One of my private clients, David, wanted to grow his company, but had a huge fear of public speaking – so, in essence, a combination of numbers 1, 2, 4 and 5. From an early age, he had traditionally avoided any possibility of speaking in public, which at school would have been, of course, very difficult to achieve. As a result, he became the quiet boy in the corner who made himself as 'grey' as possible.

So what was happening?

He was letting a seriously unhelpful series of beliefs run him. Feelings of certainty based in insecurity and inferiority that were driving unhelpful emotions, behaviour and results. As we know, 99% of these beliefs were not based in fact, but in supposition, generalisation, delction and distortion, based upon fragments of information from the world around him.

He got by, of course, but it could have been SO much easier – and happier.

It was only many years later, when he started studying in the field of mindset, that he understood that the beliefs (and therefore the emotions, behaviour and results) he had held about himself for all these years were a) not factual, b) a choice and c) therefore instantly changeable!

As a result he came up with two new habits. The first was to raise awareness of his daily thought patterns and to make a mental note to interrupt the negative belief cycle whenever he started to descend into negativity. The second was to build a robust set of alternative beliefs based upon his positive, uplifting life experiences. The trick then was *consciously* to use positive self-talk affirmations to replace the repetitive unhelpful ones.

For example, one of his most resilient and hard to break negative thought patterns was 'you've lost too much time and you've wasted your life'. Whenever he caught himself in this pattern, he would snap his fingers as a 'pattern interrupt' and then quietly affirm 'everything happens for a reason; learn from this, you can do anything you want with your life'. Another one was 'you've disappointed people so much that no one believes in you'.

David consciously sat down and wrote a list of all the great things that he had achieved in his life and so when he was caught up in this particular thought pattern, he would remind himself of the times when he had won school prizes, or when he had been proud of himself, and he would then affirm this to himself instead.

It really does work. Think about this from your perspective.

Overcoming our habitual negative self-talk and habitual limiting beliefs

Because our lives are conditioned from an early age to look at the negative, it's easy for our daily routines to throw up persistent negative mantras, or 'truths' that we tell ourselves and therefore believe to be true. Do any of these 'truths' sound familiar?

- Feelings of inferiority because of lost opportunities

- Times from the past where you have been criticised about your intelligence, judgment or ability, which you have quietly agreed with in the past and still believe

- Past failures which haunt you systematically and which therefore affect your current performance

And to counter these negative belief patterns, here are some positive alternatives with which to remind yourself whenever you find yourself slipping into old habits:

- Remember times when you overcame serious challenges

- Remember times when you were admired by others

- Remember times when you overcame your fears

- Remember times when you were proud of yourself

Don't you think it would make a difference if you made a habit of reminding yourself of your successes instead of the limiting alternatives?

Reframing: The Silver Lining

In addition to my 'toolkit' of positive self-affirmations, David also learned the trick of asking himself 'a better question' when the chips were down. What is meant by this is that he held a belief that there are positive aspects to *any* situation.

Now that's not to say that it's *always* important to try and see the advantages in any circumstances. Certain difficult situations in life, particularly in our private lives, should of course be seen with the proper solemnity and respect that they demand. What is worth remembering, however, is that it is easily possible for you to believe what is useful and empowering about:

- Your company

- Your ideas

- Your future business

- Your industry

- Your place in your industry

- Your competitors

- Your skills and abilities

- Your colleagues

…and anything else omitted from this space.

You can do this easily and quickly by reinterpreting – or reframing – your setbacks and your challenges, so that you can see them in a more constructive light. And the reason for doing this? Because change has to happen in life and you live in a world of fierce competition. The competitive advantage you will gain by getting back on track quickly and easily can't be underestimated. And in the same way that what you believe is a choice, remember this: nothing has any meaning apart from the meaning you choose to give it.

As mentioned, this is all about asking a better question.

When travelling through India on a recent business trip, Kate, a senior executive for a client of mine, left her smartphone in a taxi. It was gone. She is a self-confessed 'dinosaur' when it comes to technology and freely admits that she is perhaps not as proficient as a Gen Y individual when it comes to daily use of social media and the ever growing options/apps/chat rooms and opportunities to connect and share.

However, she lives and operates in a fast-moving global environment and she knows about the importance of online media resources, so she was more than dismayed by this oversight. What made this worse was that there was no opportunity to go to the nearest Apple store for a replacement.

Instead of going into a spin, she asked herself the question, 'What do I want instead of the problem?'

This question, seemingly simple, has a beauty about it. So simple, it is effectively a 'pattern interrupt' – in other words, like a slap in the face, it stops you in your tracks. You might be on a spiral of negativity, thinking to yourself, 'How could this have happened?' (helpful question? er, no!) or 'Why was I so stupid?' (helpful? again, no!).

The question 'What do I want instead of the problem?' forces you to think in a different way. It is impossible to think of the negative situation that has happened and instead compels us to look for a solution. So two things happen here:

1. You stop thinking in the past and think in the future.

2. You stop blaming and start thinking proactively – in other words, you are going from a negative focus to a solution focus.

It's simple but incredibly powerful.

In this instance, Kate realised that there was nothing to be done and she quickly focused on what positive steps she needed to take. She then asked herself the question, 'What could be good about this?'

Once again, the different focus that this question demands makes sure that you are focusing on the silver lining – the positive side to the challenge. In answer to this particular setback, she quickly came up with the following thoughts:

- I'm travelling through India. Not obsessively focusing on a 4x3 inch screen will allow me to look around me at the amazing spectacle of Jaipur that is unfolding around me as I float past in my ivory tower of a cab

- Whilst the mobile is a part of life these days, going without is quickly reminding me about what really matters, especially when I look around me at this vast population who have nothing and give everything

- I will back up everything from now on

- I will make sure that I spend more 'me' time in the future and less 'phone' time

It was actually a profound experience for Kate, and she realised how conditioned she had become to the unimportant things in her life, just because they were there. As she relates so passionately, it was particularly jolting in that extraordinary, vibrant, essential, life-and-death pageant of noise, colour and human drama.

The last great question to ask yourself when faced with a challenge or a setback that really resonates is 'Where else could this be useful?' Make a list of your top strengths and weaknesses and ask for feedback from people you know and trust. The list in itself is insightful, but in the case of the weaknesses, ask yourself for each one, 'Where else could this be useful?'

An example weakness might be 'being disorganised' for example.

When you ask yourself where else this could be useful, your brain is *forced* to look for an answer. It's not always immediately obvious, but once you get one, the others will become easier. An example of an answer might be in this instance: being organised means looking to the future to an extent. My disorganised side means I'm living in the present. It also means that I'm great at delegation.

Tip: If you are struggling to come up with an advantage to your 'weaknesses', use the internet and type in 'advantages of…' and you will get an answer! But try and do it by yourself first.

Ask yourself:

- What do I want instead of the problem?

- What could be good about this?

- Where else could this be useful?

Ultimately, self-belief can be equated to some degree to self-reliance. Self-reliance is the result of self-belief.

Self-reliance is largely about courage of every kind. It is not surprising that stepping on to a stage in front of a largely cynical and highly intelligent group of professionals requires courage. Remember the six fears: rejection, failure, loss, embarrassment, exposure, conflict? Pretty much all of these apply to the potential pitfalls imagined by a nervous would-be speaker.

As Brené Brown says, *'Courage comes from the Latin word meaning 'heart' – so courage can be interpreted as speaking from your heart. Courage is being willing to let go of who you feel you should be in order to be who you are.'*

Summary

The key points to take away from this crucial chapter which is all about you as a learner and an enabler for others:

- The biggest gift you can ever give yourself is a higher level of **S**elf-awareness – once you have this, everything becomes possible

- Become a subject matter expert – always look to **U**nderstand deeper distinctions about the subjects you are passionate about and create a hunger – or a **C**raving for that subject

- Cultivate a perspective of **C**ontribution – remember that when you help others, you are creating a cycle of generosity

- Remember that it won't always work first time and that persistence – or **E**ndeavour – is one of the most powerful tools you have

- Have a **S**trategy for staying aware – once you embed the habit of rejoice, reframe, refine, you will never look back

- Lastly, any successful entrepreneur will tell you that, through the ups and downs, the one thing that never left them was **S**elf-belief

CHAPTER 3
THE CONTENT

'Above all, think of life as a prototype. We can conduct experiments, make discoveries, and change our perspectives. We can look for opportunities to turn processes into projects that have tangible outcomes. Active participation in the process of creation is our right and our privilege. We can learn to measure the success of our ideas not by our bank accounts but by their impact on the world.'

Tim Brown

In this chapter we will be looking at the following:

- How to package your own expertise into your own Intellectual Property that is modular, easy to teach, easy to learn and easy to understand

- How to structure your content so that you will never be lost for words

One of the most important factors to remember is that whilst you may be superb at what you do and you are rigorous in your pursuit of excellence in your chosen field, doing it isn't the same as teaching it! It's the same scenario in most walks of life.

Neil is a senior executive and an important client. It didn't start out that way however. Maths was Neil's nemesis as a schoolboy. After keeping up with the others during the basics of adding, subtracting, multiplying and division, something missed its mark for him in maths lessons and he was seemingly one of the few boys in his class who just didn't get it. If you were to ask him about fractions or equations, you would be waiting an awfully long time for an answer!

And what made this worse was that it was clearly all his fault, not the maths teacher's. 'Pathetic' the master would say, as he handed out Neil's pitiful test results. It even got to the stage when at a parent/teacher evening, Neil's maths teacher told his father that 'hell would freeze over' before Neil passed his maths O Level.

Maths was deemed essential, especially back then, so after his first attempt at the exam ended in the miserable failure everyone expected, his parents sent him to a private tutor, who gave him four one-hour sessions, covering the main elements of non-comprehension (most of the syllabus for Neil). Neil didn't know how it happened quite so quickly, but his tutor 'opened his eyes'. In no time at all, he was asking with disbelief, 'Is that *it*?! I mean, is it really that simple?'

Neil passed his O Level with a C grade, after just four hours of tutoring. The critical factor here was the teaching methodology, which turned nine years of struggle into a 90-minute breeze. It was not a matter of intellect. His wires were just tangled, that's all. The key here was that his tutor understood how to package the key factors in as simple a format as possible, so that even he, a much-ridiculed maths dunce, saw and understood.

Neil's experience gives us two powerful lessons:

- Firstly, if there's something that isn't working, don't just keep doing it, change your approach until it does work; a new methodology may be all you need

- Secondly, try to take the phrases 'I can't' and 'it's impossible' out of your vocabulary

People learn in different ways and at different speeds. Therefore, one of the most effective tools available to anyone looking to pass on their expertise is the creation of bulletproof content that is robust enough, simple enough and packaged intuitively enough to market and to teach your products and services to *anyone*.

The key is to have a methodology that is repeatable and also flexible enough to be used in multiple ways: for example, face-to-face, on audio as well as video.

This is where most professional communicators go wrong. They may be entertaining, stimulating, even inspiring, but without a structured approach, it is all too easy to overwhelm your audience and leave them confused – and critically, disinclined to engage further.

Solution structure

There are highly successful precedents for having a simple and very effective formula. Daniel Goleman, for example, has used a 2 x 2 matrix to explain the fundamental components of Emotional Intelligence and how each quadrant interacts with each other. The key here is for highly practical yet potentially complex material to be made simple and practical through the use of the system. These systems can be hierarchical in design, such as the well-known iceberg model or the logical levels made so accessible by Robert Dilts.

A solution structure should also be a map – an easy-to-read direction finder that can navigate you from the start of the process to the end.

As mentioned, most professionals in the mentoring industry are not systematic enough in their approach, leaving their content to be taught very much on an ad hoc basis. This leaves their expertise in their heads, rather than laid out in a structured approach. The crazy thing is that these same professionals re-think the same material again and again before stepping on to a stage. As a result, they represent great value in the moment but they are not maximising what they know.

A structured, packaged and branded system of your products and services, if applicable, will enable you to teach each part of your content in a consistent way, without going off track or wondering what comes next. In addition, it also allows your audience to follow each step of the process effortlessly. The only thing you now have to do is to sit down and design your own system for your own products and services.

This is the Performance Pentagon

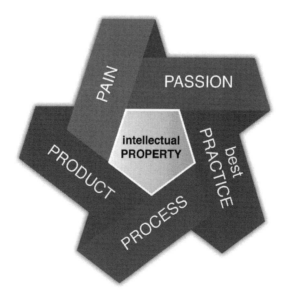

1. Pain

What is meant by this? The first step is to put yourself in your audience's shoes and consider what their challenges are – where the need, or the **P**ain, is. This will obviously depend upon the industry and/or sector in which you work. To take a topical example, your focus area might be public speaking. Your target audience, therefore, would consist of coaches, teachers, mentors, people in sales, marketing, advertising, small business owners, people who want to 'go it alone', sole traders and entrepreneurs, amongst others.

Your goal would be to understand the challenges that these people face in communicating their knowledge to the world and then to provide solutions to those challenges. In fact, you would have to dig under the surface to find out exactly what these issues were likely to be. In other words, you would have to put yourself in the shoes of your audience and diagnose their 'Pain' – and that's the first step.

For our imagined scenario, what you might come up with would be the following challenges for your target audience that would need solving:

1. There is a need to build, and then hone, **the skills needed** to command a stage and communicate with confidence and authority.

2. It's not enough just to present clearly, so next comes the **ability to engage and inspire** an audience of any size and seniority.

3. It's difficult to present and to inspire without **the right mindset** – so a toolkit of empowerment for the individual.

4. Next, the creation of a suite of products and services that is easy to understand, easy to process, easy to use and easy to remember.

5. Lastly, it's all about **maintenance and improvement**. The techniques involved in ensuring that your efforts

are always current, your products and services are not becoming outdated, and your awareness levels of your own performance are in place, so that you always perform and promote yourself and your company to its full potential.

2. Passion

This second point is a given – in a way it stands to reason that you're going to focus on things that you are passionate about. However, in many cases, it's easy to forget where your passion lies within a generalised topic. For example, in our example, public speaking covers a wide area of specialised topics. It's best to focus on the areas that you are a) best at and b) love doing.

3. Next, it's best Practice

This step is about spending some time to collate and assemble your material. The advice – or mentoring – industry has been around for many years in its varying forms and there is naturally some ground breaking and timeless material out there that is too good to be left out of your offering.

Now we need to be clear – this is not just about stealing other people's precise ideas and promoting them as your own. I would recommend instead looking at the concepts or ideas that have really resonated with you or helped in your development and then asking yourself how they can be improved. By adding or tweaking already great material, you are building on an already useful concept. So long as you are ethical in your approach, this is a great strategy.

In essence this is about the well-known fact that success leaves clues. So the strategy is to look at what currently exists 'out there' that has been successful. Much of the 'game changing' content available is actually not bound by copyright and is in the public domain. So this next stage is about sitting down and thinking about what are the best or most useful or most inspiring thoughts and ideas that you have found formative in your development as a specialist in your given area and then thinking about how you might add to them or improve them. This process is called modelling, as mentioned in Chapter 1 and is a tried and tested shortcut to achieving great results.

4. Process

The fourth part of the approach is to **P**rocess your material. Once you have become very clear about what your target audience's needs are and worked out a selection of products and services that will provide a solution for these needs (recognise your target market's **P**ain and collated all the relevant best **P**ractice of what else is 'out there'), the third step is to streamline, or **P**rocess, your offering, by adding to it all your best knowledge and skills together with your adapted version of the best products and services that have been either helpful to you in your development or that you know have intrinsic value.

5. Products

Next, you need to sort all your material into a series of products that can either work as standalone items or that fit into the rest of your offering. The key here is to understand that your selection of products needs to be ordered into a simple and intuitive order that makes learning simple. Remember Neil's maths epiphany? It all happened because the same material was presented to him in a new and simple way that he could understand.

It can't be overstated enough, the importance of *simplifying* your offering. It's the 'difference that makes the difference' when you are looking to change the way that people have historically operated. You are asking them to step outside their traditional comfort zone and to try on a completely different way of working. And it's great that they are doing that, of course, but in order to enable them to have faith, you have to sell the idea to them and this will not happen unless you can make the new methodology easy and intuitive. And for your methodology to be easy, is has to be logical and structured.

So perhaps the best way to organise your products and services into a logical hierarchy is to put yourself once again into your audience's shoes and to consider their priorities accordingly.

To make the content 'stick', you have various techniques around which to make your products and services both memorable as standalone products and services in their own right, as well as aligning themselves with your overall offering. The best way of doing this is to give them memorable names or titles which are crucial for your target audience's understanding, and here is a choice of four options:

Alliteration

You may well have heard of the adage of the Seven Ps as a method of improving your delivery: 'Prior Preparation and Planning Prevents P*** Poor Performance'.

And why?

Our brains are adept at 'pattern recognition', which is primarily a survival strategy. Our ancestors needed to adapt quickly and to recognise, for example, which foods were edible and which were poisonous. As a result, the pattern created by the use of alliteration, initially in literature and latterly in the commercial world, has become a very effective means of creating recognition for consumers.

As an example, our storytelling structure the **Ten P's Anecdote Architect** is based around alliteration:

Process, **P**icture, **P**rotagonists, **P**erson, **P**atter, **P**roblem, **P**erception, **P**lan, **P**ertinent **P**oint, final **P**erspective.

Whilst your audience may not remember every element, there is a high probability that they will recall the structure itself.

Acronyms and Mnemonics

If you are a musician, do you remember, 'All Cows Eat Grass', or for the budding navigators, 'Never Eat Shredded Wheat?' These age-old memory tools, or mnemonics, have helped us recall musical keys and the markings of a compass for as long as we can remember.

Current research says that using memory tools such as acronyms allows them to retrieve material more easily and to 'store' information more effectively. If you can make your acronym form a word that has relevance to its topic and purpose, so much the better.

Rhyme

In the same way as alliteration and acronyms, a rhyme has great 'stickability'. How many of your childhood nursery rhymes do you remember?

There are two main reasons why we remember: the rhyme and the repetition. As adults, the best example of rhymes that live with us are song lyrics, and for the same two reasons: rhyme and repetition, although with song lyrics there is an argument for an even greater retention through the addition of music.

Rhymes are great memory aids. Each line ends in a similar sound, which creates an easily remembered 'singsong' pattern. But the rhyme also helps us to encode information more easily as well. For example, you may remember history tests during your early schooldays and the penalties that may have resulted in a less than satisfactory score. This particular rhyme to remember the order of English monarchs has saved countless schoolchildren time and again.

It starts with William the Conqueror and continues to the present, but here's a small snippet:

Willie, Willie, Harry, Steve

Harry, Dick, John, Harry three

One, two, three Neds, Richard two

Harrys four, five, six, then who?

The process of learning the ability to remember and understand information learned through rhyme and hearing is highly effective and is called 'acoustic encoding'.

Structure

There are various forms of structure that are used in teaching. Structures are very effective because they allow the learner to view and assimilate large amounts of information through visual assessment. In addition, the structure itself can help get the message across.

We're using a structure example here with the IP Pentagram. The four steps to learning is another great example.

Intellectual Property

This process is in effect a checklist. As you will see from the diagram, it is only when you have all the elements in place that you can claim to have created catchy useful Intellectual Property.

You've done all the hard work: you have created all the best possible material to answer the needs of your target audience; you have assembled the information into a logical, practical and structured format; you have ensured that it is streamlined, branded and catchy.

The name you give both the individual elements of your offering need to be clear and simple as mentioned. In addition, you might want to think of an overarching name, which can encapsulate your entire service or suite of products and services. The overarching name needs to be aspirational because it should reflect both the practical application as well as the overall intent, or vision.

So, that's it. You have created a brilliant catchy system that is all your own. Just to be clear: this system will enable you to structure your speeches so that you don't need to remember where you are and, more importantly, you don't have to memorise verbatim large chunks of information and makes your delivery more conversational.

Have you ever heard the adage 'telling the truth means never having to remember what you said'? There is a difference between remembering what you said (i.e. memorising your speech) which often comes across as planned, prepared and artificial, and telling the truth – or should one say *telling your truth*.

Your authentic self on stage is what sells you because you are speaking from your heart and, as we know, people buy emotionally, not rationally. You may have great branded products, which is a fantastic start and sets you up as an authority, but unless you can access your true self – your authentic self – on stage, you're going to have an uphill struggle inspiring people. And that's what your own designed suite of products and services will give you: the confidence to engage the audience with authenticity.

Summary

In this chapter, we have looked at the ways in which you can turn what you know into highly valuable modular IP that people will pay handsomely for.

In essence, we have looked at:

- How to package your own expertise into branded Intellectual Property that is easy to teach, easy to learn and easy to understand

- How to create modular content that will inspire your audience

- How to structure your content so that you will never be lost for words

CHAPTER 4
THE AUDIENCE

'Personally I am very fond of strawberries and cream, but I have found that for some strange reason, fish prefer worms. So when I went fishing, I didn't think about what I wanted. I thought about what they wanted. I didn't bait the hook with strawberries and cream. Rather, I dangled a worm or grasshopper in front of the fish and said: "Wouldn't you like to have that?" Why not use the same common sense when fishing for people?'

Dale Carnegie, *How to Win Friends and Influence People*

In this chapter, we will be looking at the following:

- Ensuring that you are focusing in the right area

- The six steps to ensuring that everything you prepare has a customer focus, rather than a 'you' focus

Positioning yourself for your audience

Phrases like 'The customer is always right' should leap to mind when we start to think about positioning ourselves in front of our target audience. Without an audience, you have no business. There are some very enlightening statistics about the importance of customer attraction, customer service, customer value and customer retention readily available with our access to the internet.

Here are a few statistics from last year:

Customer experience

- Over 60% of consumers have cut ties with a brand over a single poor customer service experience

- Over 60% of people think that customer experience is more important than price in their choice of a brand

- Approximately 90% of consumers began doing business with a competitor following a poor customer experience

Customer loyalty statistics

- The probability of selling to a new customer is between 5% and 20%

- The probability of selling to an existing customer is between 60% and 70%

- It costs six times more to attract a new customer than to retain an existing one

- Loyal customers are worth up to ten times as much as their first purchase

This suggests just one thing: look after your customers!

Today, there's more choice, more reach, more instant gratification for pretty much any itch that needs scratching available to us all; it's much easier for us to find the solutions to our problems and so it follows then that it's much easier for us to be choosy, capricious, fussy and intolerant as clients.

The good news is that the mentoring industry is alive and thriving. The reason for this is clear: self-development, like death and taxes, is what is known as an evergreen industry. It is recession proof, which is fantastic news for anyone wishing to offer expert advice to a large number of people.

In the first chapter, we looked at the importance of having a DREAM – in other words, the decision-making ability, the purpose, the methodology, the ability to measure your progress and the ability to find a role model. As a process, it is always going to be robust and extremely helpful. None of this works, however, if you do not get your *positioning* right.

If you asked a group of people looking at the same view what they saw, would they all say the same thing? Would they see exactly what you saw? Of course they wouldn't. In the same way, we as individuals describe *our* view of the world through *our own* lens. And it's the same with most people wishing to impart expert knowledge and advice to an audience. They tend to project *their* view of the problems and challenges on to their audience through their lens of experience, without necessarily seeing the world from their audience's view.

As we have said, the 21st century consumer is picky – you can't afford to get *how* you communicate your expertise wrong. Getting into the habit of journeying through the eyes of your audience is critical and needs discipline.

The commonest and most devastating mistake you can make, which is guaranteed to alienate your audience, is to pitch your topic in either too simple or too complex a way. The first – and arguably the worse of the two mistakes – is to speak about a topic that your audience may well already know because inevitably they will feel talked down to or patronised. And if that happens, you're packing your bags.

But it's also pretty nasty when you *assume* that your audience knows or understands the material you are discussing. Inevitably, they will feel misunderstood, or confused, which has a similarly devastating result, with the only possible mitigation that you may have some goodwill left to resurrect another time.

Ideally, it's better to have actually experienced this rather than just reading and then understanding it; through experience, you will never forget the lessons learned – the more formative the lesson, the more definitive the change.

In our live seminars, we make sure that we practise the 'pitching' of subject material several times, so that our delegates have experienced the art of managing expectations and have done enough audience analysis up front, so as to make sure this doesn't happen in a real scenario.

A wonderful visual definition of empathy is 'the art of putting yourself into another's shoes'.

It's a great mental image, but quite often presents a significant challenge when people look to move from theory to practice. Of course we all 'get it' – but how do you actually put yourself in someone else's shoes?

The legendary strategist Sun Tzu quoted his famous line *'Every battle is won or lost **before** it is ever fought'* with good reason. A modern descendant of this epic line could be the well-known 'prior planning and preparation prevents particularly poor performance' that we mentioned a little while ago.

Both sayings – one classic and the other alliterative – are speaking of course of the critical importance of preparation in all things. And never were truer or more appropriate words spoken than in the case of public speaking. It is not clear as to why this happens, but the phrase 'know your audience' sets every prospective public speaker nodding in agreement; it makes perfect sense to do some audience analysis.

Why then do so few people actually do the work? So often when people put their speeches together, there seems to be a reticence to put in the hours when it comes to planning and preparation. Whatever the reason – whether it's an overall shying away from the whole process because the prospect is overwhelming, or whether it is the result of innate laziness – the fact remains that the biggest de-railer of all when it comes to catastrophe in the public speaking domain is a lack of planning.

To counter this most dire of mistakes, over the years we have gradually built up a process that makes the all-important shift from 'self' to 'audience' and ensures that you plan in the right way, every time. As a result, your communication will land in a way that is conducive to a great learning experience for all concerned.

It's called Walk Six Steps In Their Shoes

Step 1 – *Set an Objective* for Your Audience

This chapter is all about your target market – your future audience. Everything in this chapter is about the audience and from your audience's perspective.

When people prepare a speech, you might be surprised to know that most of them don't consciously set an objective at all! They just sit in front of their laptops, slowly piecing together content that they know and that they feel will be appropriate for the requested topic. Even those who do consciously set an objective for their speech will almost always do so from their own perspective. It stands to reason, right? It's my speech, so it's my objective – what's wrong with that?

What's wrong with that is that, in the same way that we project our view of the world on to the world and expect everyone to see things the way we do, so the same principle thrives here.

But if you truly want to reach and to engage your audience, the rules for setting your objective *must* change.

Instead of asking yourself the traditional, 'What's my objective for this speech?' the suggestion is to put yourself into your audience's seats and to design your speech around specific objectives that you have set with them in mind.

Here are four questions that you will find very helpful if you want to make sure your planning has a focus that will put your audience centre stage because every part of your communication will have been designed *through your audience's eyes:*

    a)   What do I want my audience to think?

    b)   What do I want my audience to know?

    c)   What do I want my audience to feel?

    d)   What do I want my audience to do differently as a result?

The first two questions, as you can see, are intended to provoke interest and new insights for your audience. Your content has to be interesting and it has to be thought provoking.

The last two questions move from the **rational motivators** of thought and knowledge to the **emotional drivers** of change and action. Our limbic, or emotional, brain controls decision making. If you can influence and stimulate your audience's emotions, new decisions and therefore new actions can and will follow.

Therefore, please don't skip this vital step of setting audience-focused objectives – it's where the magic begins.

Step 2 – *Research* Your Audience

Ask yourself the following questions:

Who am I to be talking to them?

One of the most important questions to ask yourself from an audience perspective and once again it's all about positioning. Of course you will know what you bring to the party, but building credibility and rapport at the start of your speech is as important as the subject matter itself. So, depending upon your audience's age, experience etc., you need to remember to tell them *why you are qualified* to stand there, in as contextually relevant a way as possible and as fast as possible.

Why is my subject relevant to them? Where's their pain and therefore what solution do I offer them?

A priceless question to ask yourself when looking to position your subject matter for your audience at the start of your speech.

What will they get out of my material?

This question is one of my favourites because whilst it will be perfectly obvious to you that your content and knowledge is precious, the value of your material should always be seen *through your audience's eyes*. There are almost always assumptions that we make as speakers that presuppose our audience's comprehension. Find an unbiased person to be your 'guinea-pig' and ask them to hold up their hand every time something is not clear. You may be surprised at the result. It's also a brilliant question to ask yourself with regard to the start of your speech and positioning your subject matter.

Why them and why now?

More positioning here too, in that whilst the relevance of your speech to your audience is crystal clear to *you*, it needs spelling out to *them*, and preferably near the beginning.

What is their level of understanding?

Depending upon the situation, you may either know this instinctively from the context of the event in question or be able to find out from the event organisers an idea of the demographics of your audience.

What are their key issues?

This is once again driven by the context of the situation. However, as with the previous two questions, even if you do not have all the information you require, you can always ask the audience with a 'I'm curious – can I get a show of hands if…' or a 'raise your hands if I'm right in thinking that…' question.

What do we have in common?

This is generally an easier question to either answer or find out. You will normally be making a speech in a certain place at a certain time for a reason. From that, it's a matter of simply asking yourself where the crossover lies between you and your audience. You might want to think about commonly held assumptions and beliefs as well as experience and skills that you may have in common with the audience.

What are their expectations of the presentation or speech?

Hopefully lower than the audience-focused speech that you are about to deliver.

The critical point to make here is that most speeches and presentations are ill-prepared and rarely come from the perspective of the audience; it's normally speaker focused, which should give you a huge advantage before you even open your mouth.

What is at stake?

An opportunity for you to help, guide, instruct, inspire and, most importantly, to *build trust.*

What do they value?

Audiences in general want **BALLS.** That is to say: **B**revity, **A**uthenticity, **L**aughter, **L**ight bulb moments and **S**ense – it's a great mantra to remember as a speaker.

What material should I gather as a result?

As mentioned, most speakers will not do enough due diligence on each specific audience and, as a result, the content delivered can be a hit and miss affair. So much information is now readily available online; LinkedIn and Facebook profiles which are written by the individuals themselves will give endless clues as to their preferences. Much will depend upon the accuracy of your audience analysis – that's to say, how accurately you have assessed their age/interest level/ knowledge of your subject/likelihood to buy into you and your topic etc. Once you have done this, you will be in a much better position to collate content that is a) contextual for them and b) relevant to their needs.

Step 3 - *Structure Your Speech* for Your Audience

As mentioned above, you would be amazed at the lack of preparation that goes into the standard speech or presentation, from a lack of objective setting and researching the audience. The same applies with structure.

Why structure your speech?

It stands to reason that if you can apply a framework to what you are saying, it will help the audience to follow the train of thought that you are pursuing. But more than that – much more than that – the *right* structure for the audience in hand will either inform, or persuade, or both, according to the type of speech you have in mind. The right structure will keep your audience on track and interested as we have discussed. But here's the thing: it will also keep you on track.

Imagine having a structure that allows you to respond to any change in direction that your audience demands of you, and yet ensures that you will never lose your thread, nor will you confuse your audience with the direction and flow of your material. Imagine the confidence that is generated by the knowledge that you can't get lost!

Imagine the confidence that you will feel when you realise that you don't have to learn any more lines, sure in the knowledge that the structure won't let you down.

Whilst you can't have everything and this is theory only (by the nature of its being a book), here are the basics of a great structure methodology.

You may well have heard the saying: 'Tell them what you're going to tell them, tell them, and then tell them what you told them.' A really helpful way of looking at this is to think about the TV news.

SPEECH STRUCTURE
"THE NEWS"

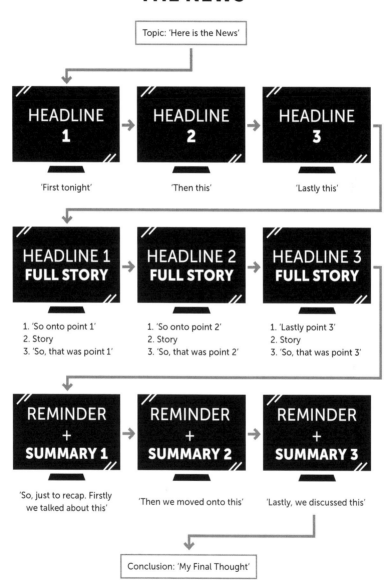

Firstly, the headlines.

Secondly, reviewing each headline in turn.

Thirdly, summarising the elements covered.

The structure used represents a fantastic way of making sure that the material is concise, hierarchical and above all, memorable.

A few key strategies are used:

    i)   The law of primacy and recency

    ii) Repetition

    iii) Conditioning

i) Primacy and recency

There's a much used phrase in the speaking fraternity, which goes as follows: 'Start strong, finish stronger.'

As humans we remember what is said at the start and we remember what is said at the end more than we remember what is said in the middle. Therefore, it is very important to make sure that what you say at the start of your speech is important (instead of 'fluff and bluster') because you can be sure that your audience's receptors are taking in much of what you are saying.

The end is much easier to remember; we all know instinctively that the end of the speech needs to contain a key message or a call to action, even if it's because it's the end! Even here, it's very surprising how often people will squander this opportunity and will 'tail off' rather than finish with a memorable 'bang'.

ii) Repetition

One of the main reasons that we remember the words of our favourite childhood nursery rhymes, not to mention our times tables from our early maths lessons, is because of the endless repetition that we used – either voluntarily in the case of the rhymes or under duress in the case of the maths!

I expect you will have heard of the 'tell them what you're going to tell them, tell them, then tell them what you told them' structure and the efficacy of this is borne out by the repetition. It just works!

iii) Conditioning

In the West, we are taught to read from left to right. This conditions us to expect a left to right format in all learning material, which is helpful when we are preparing because we can use this to our advantage. It's the same when we look through a menu: we don't start with the pudding, it's always the first course, and then the main and *then* the pudding (unless of course we are going for a shortened 'one course wonder' version).

The same applies to the structuring of our speeches. We offer the audience our speech as we would with a menu – this way, they know what's coming. After opening remarks and a little personal introduction to position both yourself and your topic, it goes as follows:

'Firstly, I'm going to talk about X, then I'm going to go on to discuss Y, and lastly I'll be discussing Z' *(tell them what you're going to tell them)*.

You then go into each of your 'menu' items in turn *(tell them)*, before summarising as follows:

'OK, so just to recap: firstly, I talked about X, which was important because... I then spent some time investigating Y and the relevance of... before finishing on the all-important topic of Z' *(tell them what you have told them)* and finishing with your concluding comments.

So this is the basic structure around which we recommend you build your speech. It should be intuitive and fit perfectly into the conditioned learning pattern of your audience. As mentioned, this is a basic structure, which will allow you and your audience to stay 'on track'.

Step 4 – *Visual Aids* for Your Audience

If there is one piece of advice around the subject of visual aids that is of most use, it has to be this: *you* are the main visual aid.

That's it.

Many people fall into the trap of creating busy slides, drawing grids on flipcharts, or creating ever more animated visual imagery, accompanied by videos, and they forget that visual aids are there to support us as speakers, rather than to be the entire focus itself. After all, if it were all about the visual aids why not just send the presentation to the audience via email?

This having been said, there are naturally times when information can be shared which supports your verbal communication. The trick is to make sure that your visual aids are just there to back you up and not the other way round.

Here are a few common sense points to remember:

- It's obvious, but make sure all aspects of technology are compatible – if you are providing the laptop, make sure you have the right adaptors etc.

- Remember the audience at all times – for example, make sure that your font is large enough so that each person in the audience can read it

- A picture paints a thousand words – stimulate your audience's imagination as much as possible using images as well as text with diagrams, pictures and photographs

- Use a variety of visual aids – e.g. flip chart *and* slides (when appropriate)

- Involve the audience – don't forget that you and the audience are the best visual aids

- Remember the B key to control the focus of the audience (I'm sure you know this, but if you press the B key, the slides will 'black out', allowing all the focus to revert to you

- Make sure that you click through the presentation in advance to make sure that there are no glitches

- In addition, ensure that you play through any videos and audio clips for video and sound quality in advance

Step 5 – *Rehearse and Test*

Statistically, rehearsal is the least practised skill of the public speaker! Quite why this should be beggars belief. Why on earth wouldn't you practise before doing something scary? There's really no excuse, especially as you can rehearse anywhere, anytime: in your car, in the shower, in bed, on the loo…

Keep yourself firmly rooted to your audience's seat as you're rehearsing your content from your audience's perspective. There are two great ways of doing this:

1. Get some objectivity, by asking for an impartial view from someone whose opinion you trust.

2. Why would your potential customers care about each element of your speech or presentation? After every point/ slide, ask yourself the question 'So what?' from the audience's perspective to test relevance.

If you give the proper focus to this step, you will probably trim your content down by as much as 40%.

Have you addressed the audience's 'pain'?

In other words, from their perspective, 'So what? Why should **I** listen to this?'

Have you included the right amount of information?

Why should I listen to **this**?

Have you provided the 'remedy' to the audience's 'pain'?

Why should I **listen** to this? Is there a logical flow to the speech? Have you removed any confusing jargon?

Are your persuasive messages clear and relevant?

In other words, 'Why should I listen to this **now**?'

Step 6 – *After Your Speech, Review!*

After the objective setting and the rehearsal, the other much-neglected must-do is the review.

As you read this, the hope is that you are instinctively agreeing with the need to review; why then do so few people make a discipline of this? Is it complacency, or is it laziness? Or is it just that people don't think about doing it?

Whatever the common reasons that others produce for not reviewing their performances, try not to follow suit if you can. The reason that we may be labouring this point is that it is impossible to improve unless you review your highs and lows after each performance.

It's *vital* to do this.

Lastly, the brain, for all its brilliance, does have its weak spots and it's too much to expect anyone to remember the minutiae of a speech, which may have occurred sometime in the past. It's therefore also vital to *write down* your findings instead of just having a think about what's just happened. Only this way can you then look back over your learning journey and read how far you have come.

Stagecraft: Make Your Content Sing for Your Audience

Ask questions (and answer them)

Once you have established your content and are enjoying the freedom of not having to remember your lines, thanks to using the Intellectual Property Pentagram Framework, the next step is to get as much engagement and buy-in from the audience as possible. You can do this using several different techniques and all based around your content and material.

The first and probably the most useful stage technique for creating buy-in is by asking questions. There are three main types of questions: closed, open and follow-up. Each of these has a specific purpose and after the ability to really listen is probably the hardest skill for the communicator to become proficient in.

After all, performance coaching, which is essentially listening and asking questions with purpose and on purpose, is a skill that takes years to learn and this is largely because there are so many very human interferences that get in the way.

Closed questions

A closed question invites either a short response, for example: 'What line of work are you in?' Or a 'yes/no' (questions beginning with words such as will, is, are, have, has, was, can, could, would, should, etc.).

A closed question has only two main functions:

1. To get clarification: 'Can I just be clear, is this what you mean?', which is very useful if you are in a Q&A session in one of your speeches and you have been asked a question that either was unclear and sends a message to the audience that you are really interested in getting clarity in order to answer the question to the best of your ability, or someone has asked you a question that needs thought and you need some time to think.

2. To get commitment: 'Would you agree if/are you happy for me to proceed with…?'

Now when you are on stage, a targeted closed question will get agreement straight away, for example: 'Would you agree with me that one of the most important skills in your professional life is being a good communicator?' This is, of course, a great way of getting your audience 'on side'.

Open questions

An open question, on the other hand, forces people to think. Open questions begin with words like what, which, why, if, describe, tell me, and how. An open question works well in different ways. It forces people to think, as mentioned, but it also taps into emotions and, as we know, people make decisions emotionally.

If you want to introduce a topic that you believe will be of value, that few people are really good at and that the audience may need to improve, for example: *Statistically, mastering nerves when public speaking is a key differentiator between success and failure as a speaker and is a very difficult skill to acquire*, I'd like you to ask yourself two questions: 'How good am I at dealing with nerves?' And 'What are my strategies?'

You are not actually looking for direct feedback here because you are about to give them the strategies they need, but it's a good way of getting the audience's mind to focus on an area that they are probably needing to improve. In this way, you are *priming* the audience.

Open questions work very well in a Q&A environment. Let's say someone has challenged you on a point. One of the best strategies is to ask an open question back. For example: 'If you would just clarify why you asked me that question?' The respondent has to think, which gives you time, but also you are putting the onus back on the questioner, which always leaves clues to the best approach with your next question or comment.

Lastly, we have the **follow-up question.**

This can either be open or closed. The essential aim of a follow-up question is to delve a little deeper into a specific area you wish to pursue.

Let's take the closed question you have asked initially: 'Would you agree with me that one of the most important skills in your professional life is being a good communicator?' That's stage one – you've got your buy-in. You then ask your follow-up question: 'That having been said, would you also agree that eye contact is one of the most important elements?' The follow-up question ensures further buy-in and enables the audience to focus on learning rather than just listening.

The key point to remember here is not necessarily just the question itself, which points the audience in the right direction, but more importantly, it's the subtext, what you are *really* saying, which is 'I am here to help; I know what I'm talking about and I know from experience that this will help you.'

Stories

We will be spending a whole chapter on the skills and tools needed for telling impactful, relevant and inspiring stories to engage your audience. The reason for this amount of focus is that stories are the best resource available to you for inspiring and engaging an audience.

Analogies

Another great way of bringing a topic to life. One of the reasons why Jeremy Clarkson has achieved a cult (albeit Marmite) following is his outrageous, on the edge and often hilarious use of the analogy. What is meant by this? An analogy is in essence a comparison. But it's a comparison often in stark relief.

One recent example he used, as he was test driving a well-known brand of performance car, was as follows:

'The air conditioning in these cars used to be like an asthmatic sitting in the dashboard blowing at you through a straw.' Or another classic, 'This car sounds like the God of Thunder gargling with nails.'

A great couple of examples of how a comparison, or analogy, can bring a topic to life. Your analogies don't have to be funny, but if they are, so much the better. Now, you may be thinking yes but Jeremy Clarkson makes millions for having a quick wit – I haven't got a quick wit. Please don't think that Clarkson just comes up with these examples, he has to sit and think about them like everyone else. The trick is in the planning.

An analogy is just another great technique for bringing your subject matter to life, by comparing or contrasting your topic with a universally understood concept.

With an activity

There are many tried and tested activity techniques that are hugely popular and very effective ways of engaging audiences. They represent absolutely bulletproof ways of managing an audience and increasing buy-in. These activities come in the shape of energisers, table exercises and metaphors.

Energisers are generally useful at the start of a session, to set the tone as well as to get people moving, the blood flowing and brains working. They are also a 'go to' technique when taking an audience through perhaps a more reflective session, where energy in the audience will naturally dip. Energisers are by definition physical activities, but they almost always involve fun and humour as well, which is why they set the tone for a session so well.

Energisers are not just stand-alone exercises that get people moving however. They have to be relevant to the subject matter in hand or the audience will wonder why you have asked them to do what you have asked them to do. There are many to choose from, all of which can be adapted to the size and context of the audience in question.

Table exercises are very much as they sound. They can be group exercises if you have cabaret or other styles of tables in the auditorium. This also presents a great opportunity for competitive exercises between tables depending on the topic of your speech.

If you have no tables, and theatre style seating, you can still get people to get into groups of three and four and thus have table exercises; the aim is to get people thinking and sharing information, which can then be built upon and facilitated from the stage.

Table exercises can involve:

- Groups of people having discussions around a topic

- 'Polling' – discussing agreement and/or disagreement about a topic

- Fact finding – idea generation

Metaphors – there are two dictionary definitions of a metaphor

The first is: *a figure of speech in which a word or phrase is applied to an object or action to which it is not literally applicable.*

For example, *We're in the same boat* is not literally applicable – you're not actually *in* a boat, of course; it just explains a shared experience in a colourful way, using a powerful image to emphasise the point. This first metaphor definition is a great way of adding impact to your content by painting really colourful pictures with words. Consider the following:

Life is a novel. We are the authors and every day is a new chapter.

People are like onions. Whenever you peel off a layer they make you cry.

One of the biggest challenges with using metaphors happens before you have even designed your content. We can limit ourselves by telling ourselves that we are not writers, that we are not creative. 'Other people can write metaphors but I can't.' Metaphors are easy once you have got over the self-limiting 'hump'; the trick is to look for connections between two completely different topics. If you think hard enough, there are comparisons to be made between almost anything and almost anything.

Let's look at an example.

In live events, you can ask delegates to think of a topic upon which they are proficient and comfortable. You then put up a slide with images of completely random items such as a motorboat, a pair of jeans, a cake, a river, a four-leafed clover. The exercise then revolves around asking your delegates to think of their topic of proficiency and liken it to one of the examples on the screen.

For example: *Admin (if that's the thing they are good at) is like a cake. You divide it into bite sized chunks and reward yourself at the same time!*

Or we might take the motorboat, as it's the first on the list: *Public speaking (if that's the thing they are good at) is like a motorboat ride: scary at first, until you get used to the rush. It can be a bit bumpy from time to time but always leaves you exhilarated at the end.*

See the difference between this and *Public speaking can be nerve wracking but it's worth it?*

The great thing is that people always do it – and do it brilliantly! It's one of the best and most energised sessions in my public speaking seminar.

So, in practical terms, the next time you deliver a speech have a think about using some metaphors to add colour, humour and vibrancy to your delivery. These can be completely random, like the pair of jeans and the motorboat, and the brain will look for the similarities between the two, or you can go for topical or current examples to make your point.

The second definition of a metaphor is: *a thing regarded as representative or symbolic of something else.*

This definition of a metaphor is terrific in a conference setting if you want to lay down a challenge, or to beggar belief, or to get people to do things that they may well (initially) believe is beyond them. It's also the most dramatic thing you can do in front of an audience as a finale.

There are various options to choose from and they are all unbeatable as a means of converting an audience, energising an audience, amazing an audience, and changing an audience's perception about what is possible. These involve asking either select members of the audience, or if desired, asking each member of the audience, to participate in:

- A fire walk

- Punching through a block of wood

- Snapping an arrow on their throat

- Performing a seemingly impossible mind-reading trick

- Achieving a seemingly impossible memory task

   …among others.

Now when you read through the list, you will see a pretty random series of activities and the word 'why?' may well be going through your head.

There is, of course, no value in walking over red-hot coals, snapping a real arrow using the soft part of your throat, or even memorising huge amounts of seemingly useless data.

There is, however, MASSIVE value in thinking about whatever holds you back in your life and using the metaphor of something seemingly impossible, such as one of these challenges, as a comparison.

Having stepped up and snapped the arrow, or performed the mind-reading, or punched through the wood, and likened it to that life challenge, the brain is an organ of possibility and it will make the same conclusions: i.e. I've actually *done* that! Hang on – what else can I do?

To use a personal example, I have seen more personal breakthroughs as a result of people proving to themselves that they *can* do whatever has defeated them thus far than anything else and, together with personal interventions, this has generally happened at the metaphor stage of my events.

Set-ups and debriefs

There is very little point in delivering a speech if you are not looking to either educate, or sell a product, service or idea. The concept of set-ups and debriefs is simple enough and just requires planning.

First, the set–up

With a good set-up, what you are actually doing is as follows:

1. You manage expectations. If you are going to speak about a subject, the set-up will let the audience know what is in store. It's a little bit like a menu – they know what they are getting and they also know what they are *not* getting. By setting up a topic, it's all about what you are really saying which is 'I know that this topic might be scary/inappropriate/ risqué/ confusing, but I *promise* you I will make sure you're OK with this by the end.'

2. You set boundaries. If you are speaking on a detailed subject, it really helps to clarify your subject matter in advance. Your audience can know how many points there are and how long it will take and what the session will actually require of them.

Next, the debrief

One of the most common mistakes that speakers make is to stay in their own head and forget about the audience's journey. What we mean by this is that if the speaker stays 'internal', they naturally understand every point and reference that they are making. They don't need to explain anything at the end because it's all as clear as day to them.

What speakers often forget is that the subject matter they are discussing, whilst familiar territory to them, may well be virgin territory for their listeners. Far better to overexplain than not to explain at all. So, a couple of important points to remember about the importance of a good debrief:

1. A debrief will give your audience the opportunity to reflect and consolidate the knowledge you have shared and to ask questions if necessary.

2. A debrief will allow you to ask the audience to bear with you while you take them on a journey by means of a story or an activity, without necessarily setting up the exercise in advance. You can do this with no explanation at all to begin with. This suspension of understanding can often be an absolutely brilliant way of using the debrief as a punchline, or a means of explaining why you have taken them through a seemingly abstract or unrelated topic, story or activity with a real light bulb of understanding at the end.

If you can master the art of the set-up and the debrief, it will change your life as a speaker. As mentioned, this is not rocket science, but it does take planning and preparation.

Share your beliefs

This last point may sound obvious, but it's a great one. You have done all the work – you have an audience in front of you. Try not to make the mistake of being a pale imitation of other people. Tell it how you see it.

Summary

- Your audience has high expectations, low attention span and is fickle – it will drop you unless you can show you understand its 'pain', provide a 'remedy' to that pain, with great customer service at the same time

- Get 'into the zone'

- ALWAYS plan from your audience's perspective using the Six Steps In Your Client's Shoes

- Stay aware of your audience's needs at all times

- Lastly, we have included a variety of techniques to ensure engagement and buy-in from your audience at all times

CHAPTER 5
THE STORY

'Words are how you think.
Stories are how you link.'

Christina Baldwin

In this chapter we will be looking at the following:

- The incredible power of storytelling and the science that supports the argument

- A foolproof methodology of identifying and decoding your personal experiences into great story content

- Lastly, a 'one-size-fits-all' structure around which to build your content

The critically important art of positioning yourself as a credible subject matter expert and a 'go to' authority in your field has several options, and for many, there is a growing conviction that the most compelling of these is the art of storytelling.

It is fascinating to see the difference between a good speaker and an average one. The consensus is that the difference that makes the difference in being affected emotionally by a speaker is their ability to connect emotionally with the audience by means of stories.

One of the great innovators in the field of personal development, Dale Carnegie, was evangelistic about storytelling as a means of conveying emotion as well as data to his audiences, a conviction that has been proved right, especially over the last decade, where we have made more strides towards understanding the human brain than in the entire previous existence of mankind.

The advent of neuroscience and the creative use of MRI (Magnetic Resonance Imaging) brain scanning has allowed scientists to view brain activity during various communication scenarios, where remarkable results, in the storytelling process as much as anywhere else, have shown just how effective a communication skill the art of storytelling actually is.

Scientists at Princeton University in the USA found that when brain activity was observed during a storytelling process, two remarkable things happened.

1. The normal 'data transfer', or sharing of information in a logical sequence, is our traditional form of communication. In this instance, the neo-cortex, or rational, thinking brain is traditionally stimulated alone.

2. In the case of storytelling, however, other areas of the brain would also 'light up', thereby indicating that when a story is told, we are both giving and receiving information using more of our brain than we would normally use.

The brain of the storyteller was carefully monitored together with the brain of the receiver, and what was fascinating to the scientists was the fact that exactly the same areas of the brain in the listener were stimulated as the communicator – a harmony, or joining of brain activity in fact.

Using a modern idiom, this could be described as a 'brain Bluetooth'. So we have discovered that storytelling is not merely an interesting form of communication, but it also stimulates the brain more than normal communication does *and* there is this harmony – or brain Bluetooth.

Storytelling, in fact, has *teeth*!

Most of us can associate either with the bargaining tool our parents may have used on us to soften the blow of having to go to bed, or perhaps more recently, if you are a parent, you will recall using the bargaining power of a promised story for your children: 'If you're in bed in five minutes, I'll tell/read you a story.'

And it worked, did it not?

Bedtime stories are for most people some of their favourite childhood memories. And they landed all the better when told by someone who would use characterisation, accents and the full expressive range of volume, pitch, pause and modulation – the 'light and shade'. The better the storyteller, the more engaged we were.

And it wasn't just a story, we were living the adventure, going on the journey with the characters. It's a means of transporting the listener emotionally as well as rationally. The reason why Harry Potter has been so amazingly successful is because JK Rowling could spin such a good yarn that a whole generation of children the world over don't just want to enjoy the stories, they want to be the characters! Merchandising spin-offs valued at £1bn reinforce the mania.

Now remember JP Morgan's conviction that people buy into things emotionally, even though they may justify their decision rationally. The emotional connection of your audience with your communication is a thing beyond price.

So why is storytelling in business not commonplace?

In early civilisation, right through to the Middle Ages when the printing press was created, we lived by word of mouth. We learned trades, customs, laws and skills through word of mouth alone. Towns were created largely as meeting places where we could catch up on the latest news. Town criers were the bloggers, the social media and the newsreaders of their time.

In our modern society, we adore stories as children and we still learn at our mother's knee; as teenagers through to adulthood, we engage with stories all the time when people ask us 'how did it go?' or 'what happened?'

Whenever we watch movies or TV dramas, we are neck-deep in stories. They form a big part of our daily fabric and yet we see storytelling in business as an esoteric art.

We are in fact natural storytellers, but we are reticent to learn them as a business tool because that's not what businesspeople do, even though we don't realise that we tell stories about ourselves in interviews, or that every time we enter a pitch process, we are storytelling about our company!

In fact, it is our business culture that confines us

Whether you are a business owner, or an employee, or a sole trader who has worked with others in the past, it's worth bearing in mind that when we work with others and engage in our day-to-day business activities, what we are most eager to do is to follow the crowd and learn the culture of the environment we are in. The reason for this is because 'fitting in' is what we have been trained to do as children and through our adolescence.

It's much too painful to stand out, to be individual, and many of us have learned to our cost what it is like to be the odd one out, either at a party, in a social gathering or maybe even as the new boy or girl in a class. We look to find our 'set' as soon as possible and to blend in, so as not to attract too much attention.

More often than not for most people, this happens also when we make a presentation or a speech. We try to rely purely on the information we are looking to share and because it's an alien experience, we look to make ourselves as unnoticeable as possible.

This is what lies behind people speaking too fast or wandering about or mumbling or not holding eye contact. But that's for later (Chapter 6). In the cultural banana skin of communication, we become conditioned to piece together PowerPoint slides, to use data as our main focus and forget about the human element in our interaction. We forget that our communication is all about the ease for the listener and not the ease of the communicator.

We assume that stories have no place and we do what everyone else does. We go into PowerPoint mode – the death by PowerPoint experience that we all know and hate. But this dislike of being droned at and bored by slides we can't read hasn't been enough to stop it happening. The culture of 'that's what goes on around here' continues – and so does the old style of public communication.

And the rationale for the culture itself?

On the surface, we hear *rational* explanations, such as: 'There's a sound structure to knowledge sharing which is time-honoured and proven. It works. If it ain't broke, don't fix it.'

Or: 'Moreover, this is a place of serious business. Storytelling and soft skills have their place of course, but you need to get your point across in a way that businesspeople will understand.'

If we've heard storytelling described as 'touchy feely' once, we've heard it a hundred times.

There was recently a plenary workshop for 200 at a partner's conference for one of the 'big four' professional services organisations, where public speaking was on the agenda. The speaker introduced the topic of storytelling and at once there was a pin-striped arm in the air, with the question: 'Storytelling? Can I ask why we're doing this? We're not in sales or advertising. It's a waste of our time.'

The delegates were seated at round tables in cabaret style and as the spokesman sat down, he received conspiratorial grins from his colleagues and even a pat on the shoulder from one of them. He was asked a question in return: 'Can I just clarify with you why you think that this is a waste of your time?'

There was a pause, the challenger had clearly thought he could 'hit and run' without having to enter into dialogue. But to give the person handing out the hand-held microphone their due, they wouldn't let this gentleman off the hook and patiently waited for him to get to his feet again.

His response, when it came, was worth waiting for! A pearl without price: 'We work for a living here – we tell stories to our kids when we get home.'

Quite a response.

The response from the speaker was:

1. Acknowledge - *always* acknowledge

'I appreciate your comments and your concern. I also appreciate that you are experienced businesspeople with much to do.'

2. Ask another question

'If I could give you a simple strategy which would always engage your audience, whatever the size and level, might that be worth ten minutes of your time?'

3. Make your suggestion and seek buy-in

'Might I ask that you give me this short time to introduce storytelling as a core skill of a leader in this industry – or any other, for that matter – and if you still feel that this topic is a waste of time at the end, please feel free to heckle!'

A great example, amongst many examples, of a reference to how storytelling in a business context is still being viewed as alien, and whilst the objection was fluently dealt with, it outlines how old habits die hard!

The suggestion is that the reason the cynical response occurs is that people who have not tried it before will belittle it because:

That's not the way we do things around here

It happens because they spend their lives being sceptical, and if you practise anything regularly enough it becomes a habit. Scepticism breeds wariness, which in turn demands hard data to be convincing. Bear in mind too that scepticism, whilst a human characteristic and therefore to be found everywhere, is also nowhere more clearly seen than in the financial services and accounting world, where scepticism is not only a characteristic, it's quite often a job requirement.

It's not serious and business *is* serious.

It's not a logical A+B=C process

There is an abundance of the 'if you can't measure it, it doesn't exist' thinking in the business world. As a result, people will quite often feel that they can't get good at this without major effort.

Effort means change and change breeds insecurity

People are naturally reticent to change, as we know. They often feel that they haven't communicated like this before, and they are worried that they will get laughed at – a catastrophe for anyone who has spent years building a reputation for sober consideration and good judgment.

It also breeds fear

Worse still than this, if you have an audience of senior or experienced professionals, who are known and respected for what they do, the biggest fear of all is that they worry that they won't be any good at this new skill and their reputation for standing out will be lost.

*'The one part of us that keeps us out of connection
is our fear that we're not worthy of connection.'*

Brené Brown

So here's the thing...

If you want to make your mark, to engage your audience – or any audience for that matter – you have to reach their hearts as well as their minds. We know that science tells us it works and we know instinctively that we love a good story, that we are engaged and transported by a good one. The only thing to do now is to *get good!*

A story, engagingly and relevantly told, can persuade even the most hardened and cynical mind. It was apparently Dr Seuss who said, '*Why try to fit in when you were born to stand out?'* Whether he was the originator or not, the sentiment is bang on because it challenges the cultural norm. And that's exactly what storytelling does as well.

So how do I stop myself from doing what everyone else does?

Cultural conditioning swamps everything else, it is said. So the key here is to switch off your autopilot, to attune your mind, and every time you hear someone say 'that's what we do around here' or words to that effect, remember to challenge the custom in your mind for reason and practicality. It's called a 'pattern interrupt'.

Do you remember the RAS – or Reticular Activating System that we mentioned earlier? Your brain's natural focus puller? The means of connecting the unconscious mind with the conscious one? If you set yourself a conscious goal, your brain will be attuned to that goal, even while other things are going on around you. So if you set your RAS to become aware of conditioned responses, a little bell will go off in your conscious mind whenever it happens. The only trick is that you need to keep reminding yourself – this is where the phrase 'note to self' comes from!

What might stand in my way?

It's all very well your talking about storytelling, but I'm not sure I've got any stories

The art of storytelling at its best is a very personal journey. When you look back at the speeches you may have heard in your time, both professionally and personally, the very best ones, the ones that stand out, the ones that may have stuck in your mind, have been the ones that have contained personal, relevant and powerfully emotive stories. Now that is not to say that storytelling as part of the speechmaker's art needs to be depressingly sad, extraordinary or far-fetched. There are extraordinary personal stories that happen to everyone on a daily basis.

The rest of this chapter, therefore, is based upon two critical storytelling processes:

1. The **SELL** – a means of identifying and then decoding your own personal experiences into compelling material for your stories.

2. The **Ten P's Anecdote Architect** – a bulletproof storytelling superstructure which will ensure that your personal experiences entertain, inform and inspire your audiences every time.

Cast your mind back over your past, to the events that have happened which have shaped you. It's guaranteed you that you will have some absolute belters in there!

As a framework, to help filter these stories and their relevance, ask yourself the following questions and make some notes, using the following technique for generating the stories from your life:

What's your SELL?

Struggle – Think about the challenges, conflicts or difficulties you may have had in your life. These struggles can either be internal struggles or external ones – or both. We have all been through the emotional mill, but at this stage, remember that a good story is all about the journey from status quo, through pain and struggle to enlightenment, so to begin with I want you to focus on the adversity you have had in your life thus far. Try and think of five examples if you can and don't worry about their relevance or how this will work at this stage.

- What were the biggest lessons of my childhood/adolescence/adulthood?

- What do I remember about my rites of passage? (first time away from home/first time I went camping/first kiss/school memories/learning to drive etc.)

- What have my biggest challenges been growing up?

- What have the biggest challenges been in my work life?

- Where have I really struggled in my personal life?

Event – For every example that you have thought of there is always a specific challenge or memorable event associated with each. So let's say for example that one of your conflicts was people 'putting you down' or trying to undermine you. It's time for you to think about what the specific challenge or event was in each of these situations. So in the example mentioned above, it might be: 'On this one occasion, John stood up in the office and told everyone who would listen about my failure to…'

Try and think of the *specific factors involved* in each scenario from the first category you have thought of – that's the **S**truggle. The aim here is to think of the specifics of the situation and what then happened during this critical point in the story.

Once you have generated lots of examples from your specific **S**truggles and the specifics of each scenario – the '**E**vents' – try and follow this process. Go back over them and ask yourself the question: Why was that? In other words, if we take the first one – What are the biggest lessons of my childhood/ adolescence/ young adulthood? – then ask yourself *why* these stories remain with you or come to mind so strongly. It's the 'why' that is the interesting part. You may have had some fascinating scenarios, but unless you can explain why they resonate with you, leave them out.

Learning – This process, of finding the 'why' for each example, will really help you with the critical third element of the storytelling generator – the **L** – or **L**earning, where you discover a new perspective or understanding from each scenario. In effect, this is the main reason why you are telling the story in the first place.

So for each of the examples in the **S**truggle and the **E**vents categories, I want you to build upon your **L**earning specifics that you had as a result. So, to be clear, ask yourself: What did I learn from this memory? What was the lesson? By doing this, you are highlighting not only the reason for the story but also why this is relevant to what you are talking about.

Link – Lastly, and absolutely critical to the storyteller's art, is the ability to link the content of the story with the enlightenment and new beliefs held as a result of the experience.

So start becoming aware of the stories that are happening around you, both to you and to others in your sphere that happen every single day, for exactly the same reasons as above. If you can gather stories that are current, topical and relevant to your subject, you are well on your way and ahead of most of the speakers, mentors and coaches I have seen and heard on my travels.

As we've mentioned, set your RAS and make a daily 'note to self' to do this.

A great story will do four things:

1. As much as anything else it will position you as a trusted source of knowledge in your field.

2. It will create interest in the subject you are talking about.

3. If it is told right, it will engage your audience on an emotional level.

4. It provides a lesson or moral.

So, to re-cap:

We have talked about the scientific proof that storytelling engages others and creates a synergy, or 'brain Bluetooth'.

We have looked at how we as humans love stories but don't use them in business.

We have talked about conditioned behaviour, which stops us from breaking the mould and telling stories in a business context.

Lastly we have looked at ways in which we can start to focus on the stories in our lives as a means of building credibility and trust, interest and engagement, as well as providing the valuable take-away.

The storytelling process

The next step is to think about the storytelling process itself.

First, some ground rules:

Vulnerability

The emotional engagement from an audience's perspective comes from the reflections of the speaker, but it's a common understanding, resonance or empathy with the speaker that creates the emotional link. In order to create this, you need to be vulnerable.

Now just to be clear, vulnerability is NOT about weakness. We are talking about the ability to be open, honest and frank about your experiences, your struggles and the lessons that you have learnt. In fact there is great strength in being vulnerable and it's *because* of that openness and candour.

Vulnerability doesn't have to include earth-shattering or horrific experiences; it's more about finding the courage to share truthful personal reflection and learning from challenging situations and is absolutely critical when learning the art of storytelling.

Live the dream

Next, you need to help your audience *live* in the story – it's not enough just to describe the action. You need to paint a picture that is vivid and that sings. There are several ways of doing this.

If you imagine that you are a film director, you have two main channels to use: sight and sound. Think of the options you have in each of these to create emotional engagement with your audience:

Vision: Wide angle / close up / black and white / colour / sepia / special effects / action

Sound: Silence / music (think Jaws!) / sound effects

There are others, of course, but the main elements are here. And is it not true that this is how the film director creates the magic and draws us in? If it were just the story itself, even the best plot won't get the job done; it needs help and this is where you as the storyteller come in.

First, the vision element

How do you take these very effective screen techniques and use it on the stage to help *your* audience live the scene?

There are two main techniques: visualisation and body language.

Visualisation

Firstly, you need to get your audience to *visualise* your story. Over the last 30 years or so, visualisation has become a very popular technique, pioneered in the fields of therapy and NLP. It's not rocket science – in fact, if you can close your eyes and imagine your front door, you can visualise! It's a gift that we all possess because we think in pictures and self-talk, as mentioned earlier.

The key, once again, is to ask your audience, literally, to picture the scene and to help them with carefully crafted imagery. This of course takes planning and practice – you can't just rock up and 'wing it'.

Physical mimicry (body language)

For actors, the best exponents of physicality and body language, much of their training is centred on the body and use of the body as a brilliant means of 'getting into character' and associating with the characters they are playing. They are the best storytellers because their body language is telling the story for them.

Remember Mae West? Her famous quote, *'I speak two languages – body and English'* was synonymous with her certainty that people remember and associate more with body language than with anything else. Remember too that, as the human race, we were using body language for millions of years before we uttered a sound and this is still hard-wired into our psyche.

Many stand-up comedians also know the power of using body language to tell a story. They know what works and what doesn't because despite looking and sounding conversational and 'off the cuff', stand-up comedians tend to practise what they say and what they do obsessively to achieve that 'spontaneous' impression.

Your audience will follow your body language more than anything you say. Therefore the more you can inhabit the characters, the more associated with your story your audience will be. We shall be going into more detail about some great body language strategies in my delivery techniques in the next chapter, but for now, just remember that the more you can help your audience connect with your story, the more they will connect with you and your main messages.

Secondly, the sound element

There are two main uses for employing sound to engage your audience: first multi-sensory language, and second the creative use of voice.

Multi-sensory language

We all have visual, auditory (hearing) olfactory (smell) and kinaesthetic (feeling) senses, which respond to a well-told story. What is important to remember is that we also all have sensory preferences. In other words, we all have a sense that dominates the others. Our preference tends to show up in the language we use and conversely will respond better to language that defers to our preference than to others. That's not to say that if our dominant sense is visual we are oblivious to the use of auditory, kinaesthetic and olfactory descriptions – far from it. It's just that we like to be communicated to in the way that we like to receive information.

Now if you have an audience of more than one person, there is every chance that you will have different sensory preferences to communicate with. The answer: multi-sensory language. As with the descriptive language example above, you can craft your speech using all four sensory predicates, which will enable you to please all the people all the time.

This is simpler than it sounds – or looks! or feels! When crafting a story, just remember to use descriptions that will help your audience to live in the scene. When you are scene setting, for example, describe your environment and characters visually and remember to also describe the sounds of that environment, the language your characters use (another great reason for dialogue) how you and they feel/felt about the situation you are describing and remember too that many of your descriptive scenarios will also benefit from references to the smells – good, bad and awful – that may be associated to your story.

This is not to say that you have to tick each sensory box all the time, but just be mindful that a nod to each sensory preference as you go along will help to keep all of your audience engaged, not just the ones who correspond to your personal preference.

Creative use of voice

For a detailed look at the various vocal techniques you can use to engage your audience, please see the next chapter.

Structure – the 10 'P's Anecdote Architect

Lastly – and certainly as importantly as anything else – you need to structure your story so that two things happen:

1. Your audience can go on the journey without getting lost or sidetracked.

2. You can remember the story effortlessly.

Let's look at the **Ten 'P's Anecdote Architect** as our storytelling structure.

Process, **P**icture (**P**hysicals), **P**rotagonists, **P**erson, **P**atter, **P**roblem, **P**erception, **P**lan, **P**ertinent **P**oint, final **P**erspective.

The important elements of the art of storytelling lie in these letters.

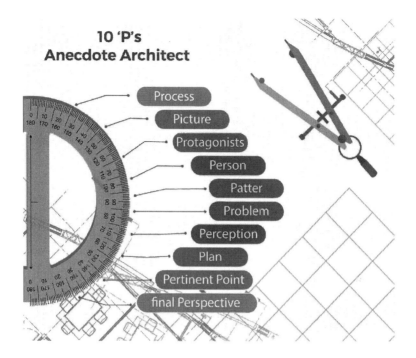

Process

First of all, you need to associate your audience with the relevance of your story and you need a **P**rocess for doing this. There are various methods:

- Question: quite often, the best way is to ask a question. For instance, if you wish to tell a story about the value of listening to others, you might pose a question like 'How many people here are good listeners?' Firstly, this will give you a good indication of how realistic your audience is (statistically, most people are worse at listening than any other communication skill) and secondly, and most importantly, what you are really saying is 'I want to talk about listening skills.'

- Statistic

- Get the audience to do something

- A strong quote

- Refer to a topical or current event

Picture

Next, you need to set the scene and describe the situation, so that there is context for your audience. If you dive straight into the action without understanding why, your audience will struggle to follow your story. Probably the best way to do this is to ask the audience to **P**icture the scene. You can do this by literally saying 'picture the scene' or words to that effect. 'Imagine, if you will…' is another good one, or to inject immediacy, dive straight in with 'OK, so it's December last year, it's 15 degrees below zero and I'm at this convention in Chicago…'

Protagonists

In the setting of the scene, remember to introduce the characters, or **P**rotagonists, as you go.

Person

It's also a good idea to decide which **P**erson you are going to tell the story from. The first person (i.e. from the 'I' and 'me' perspective) is often the most popular technique and will resonate with the audience if it is a story that contains real struggle. Remember too that you also have the third person as an option (third person speaks from a narrative point of view – e.g. 'There was a man who…'). This technique is great if you want to tell a story with a wider reference – like a global story with a moral at the end.

It's also particularly powerful if you wish to tell a personal tale in an impersonal or objective way. Quite often, it is possible for a personal story to sound too self-indulgent if it is told from a personal perspective all the way through. A story which talks about 'an individual' who goes through an extraordinary journey but who emerges at the end can often engage the audience without asking them to feel sorry for you. If you then reveal yourself as the main character at the end, the emotional reflections about the journey and the lessons learnt can all be left to the audience's individual perspectives.

Remember, as you go, to describe the characters using the **P**hysical senses of visual, auditory, kinaesthetic and olfactory as described above.

Patter

Remember too that the more conversation and dialogue, or **P**atter, you can use as a part of your story, the more it will come to life as a real event for your audience. There's realism, an earthiness and immediacy about relating actual dialogue as opposed to using pure narrative. It brings characters to life in a way that is impossible with narrative alone, as *what* people say, together with *how* they say it is within your grasp as a speaker and it gives your characters identities and personality.

Problem

Once you have explained the relevance of your story, you have set the scene and introduced the characters, there has to be a struggle. If it's all plain sailing, there's no point in telling the story in the first place. So, the journey continues with a challenge, or **P**roblem, for our main protagonist, or hero. Remember, this can be either internal, external, or both.

Perception

As you describe the situation, remember to relate the story and the emotions involved through the eyes of your main character. The climax of the story, the revelation, or **P**erception, of your main character is critical here because his or her thoughts and revelations at this form the whole basis for the story in the first place.

Plan

Inevitably, this forms the climax of the story, and for this to happen there has to be a solution, or a **P**lan, some behaviours that happened after the perception. So make sure you are clear about the sequence of events and communicate these clearly.

Pertinent Point

Lastly, every good story needs to have a moral or a key learning, otherwise the whole process has been a waste of time. The learning, or **P**ertinent **P**oint, needs to encapsulate the lesson that the main character (probably you) has learnt as a result of the journey.

Perspective

The lesson has to be rooted in conviction and come from your **P**ersonal **P**erspective.

Bringing It All Together – A Practical Example

How might you bring this all together? Here are some scenarios.

*So, how many of you out there have suffered from nerves when it comes to public speaking in the past? (*question*)*

Or:

*There was a global survey conducted some years ago into mankind's greatest fear. The response – public speaking. (*statistic*)*

Or:

*Mark Twain said: 'There are two types of public speakers: those who are nervous and those who are liars.' (*quote*)*

(Process)

The reason I ask is that I'd like you to picture, if you will, a lecture hall at Loughborough University filled with 800+ members of the Inland Revenue, good and true. **(Picture)**

The hall's not raked, so if you are standing at the front, it would be very hard to see, let alone communicate with those at the back. **(Person)**

The section chief – let's call him Ken – a fifty-something gentleman with well-worn shoes and a well-worn expression behind thick bifocals is breathing heavily as he steps up to address the audience. **(Protagonists)**

There's no air conditioning, the hall is full of bodies and is a little… ripe. The audience slowly quietens down to an expectant murmur as Ken raises a shaky hand in the air for silence.

He's perspiring, and seems to be quivering slightly and the paper he holds in his hand is fluttering like a flag in a gale. What's more, his opening salvo misses its mark quite dramatically: **(Physical senses)**

'Great to see you all here…mumble, mumble…a crossroads for HMRC… mumble, mumble…I have a couple of points to make before…'

'SPEAK UP KEN! CAN'T HEAR YOU!' comes a roar from the back. **(Patter)**

The unfortunate Ken goes bright red and beads of sweat can clearly be seen starting from his forehead. He tries again until it soon becomes clear that, whilst the Inland Revenue may be great at tax, their organisational skills are sadly lacking as they have forgotten to install any AV. Ken's friend at the back roars out more encouragement, 'STILL CAN'T HEAR YOU KEN!'

Poor Ken is forced to resort to a shout as he breaks the news that, due to cuts, every occupant of the room is sadly in danger of losing their job. His parting yell to the group informs them that to cheer them up, a motivational speaker is about to take them through a session on resilience.

The speaker in question marches in, full of beans, a tall, smiling individual, bursting with energy.

His hands are shaking so much that he has decided not to do any work with a flipchart in this session and he is replaying the words of his mentor (with whom he has been on the phone just moments before) in his head: 'fake it till you make it.' He is going over the flow of the session in his head and is determined not to let the audience know that this is his first ever professional engagement.

He tries not to look flustered as he realises that not only is there no amplification, which means an hour of yelling, but also there is no stage, so the 300 people towards the back of the room can't see him, or he them. **(Problem)**

Faced as he is with this communication dilemma, coupled with his inner battle with not so much butterflies as a flock of screeching seagulls doing battle in his stomach, it would be hard to think of a more challenging situation.

The same helpful delegate from before now gives our hero a 'nudge', 'GET ON WITH IT THEN!'

A ripple of laughter and an expectant hum accompanies this, as the more raucous members of the audience sense blood in the water. Our young speaker is only too aware that time is short before he loses control. **(Perception)**

There's only one thing for it; he pulls one of the spare folding chairs from the side of the hall, opens it with a loud clatter, steps up on to its rickety and creaking seat and proceeds with his speech. **(Plan)**

As a result of this rather eccentric decision, the speaker holds the attention of the audience for the next hour. This small victory is partly as a result of his unique and unsteady podium and the 'will he, won't he?' nature of his having to fight for his balance constantly; mercifully, it is also partly due to the topical nature of his speech.

At the end, the speaker receives a generous hand from the audience who are aware that the circumstances have been pretty tough. The speaker breathes an inward scream of relief as he walks out of the hall unscathed.

As he drives back to base in London, he reflects that there are two things that have seen him through this baptism of fire. **(Pertinent Point)**

Firstly, he realises that he has managed to think clearly even when the pressure has been intense. He thinks it's luck rather than skill, but is grateful that he has proved this to himself. Secondly, he is pleased with the fact that he kept going, even when every nerve was screaming at him to run. He is mindful of a book he has been reading called 'Feel the fear and do it anyway' by Susan Jeffers.

The name of the speaker? Oliver Medill.

I firmly believe that when public speaking, or 'mankind's greatest fear' as we now know it, the most important thing that you have to remember is that, if you've done your homework and you know your stuff, trust yourself and back yourself. **(Personal Perspective)**

So we now have a great story structure, built robustly around the **Ten P's Anecdote Architect.**

All you now have to do is to construct your own and practise, practise, practise!

A couple of other points to consider

One of the most important things to remember when telling a story is that your audience has a short attention span and will bore easily. This being the case, you need to grab their attention straight away.

This you can do in two ways:

1. Try telling your story in the present tense, for example: 'I'm attending a conference and it's the middle of the afternoon...' The present tense is a good way to bring immediacy and energy into your story. It is not always appropriate; for example, there may well be an advantage in using the past tense if you are talking specifically about the past, for example: 'On my fifteenth birthday, something happened to me that...'

2. Try starting your story in the heat of the action, where it's most exciting or noteworthy. You can then track back and forwards to reveal the set-up and the moral. The key thing is that you will grab your audience's attention by presenting them with immediate drama, rather than a slow build-up which, especially after lunch, will test your audience's attention levels sorely.

Summary

We have looked at the various ways in which storytelling can make a huge difference to your audience by focusing upon:

- The science that backs up the conviction that storytelling creates rapport and 'buy-in'

- What stops us from storytelling

- How to create compelling stories from your own experience using the Alphabet Story Finder

- How to structure a story, using the Ten P's Parable Planner

- Ways to keep the audience totally engaged with a great story

CHAPTER 6
THE MASTERY

'90% of how well the talk will go is determined before the speaker steps on the platform.'

Somers White

In this chapter, we will be looking at the critical skills you will need for 'making it happen' in front of a live audience.

Delivery

It may seem strange to you that we have looked through all these other elements of your new business approach without addressing the fundamental ingredient: the coal face! The public speaking delivery itself.

This rationale is founded upon the belief that there are many books out there which cover the fundamentals of public speaking. If we had started with the 'this is how you speak in public' bit, those feeling that the skills to speak are all that are required may have overlooked much of the other differentiating material.

That is not to say that the delivery skills are of secondary importance. This is not in any way true.

In this chapter, we will be covering some of the key skills and distinctions required to make a huge difference when speaking in front of an audience, some of which may not be covered in other publications.

In our live seminars, we will always make sure that everyone is on a 'level playing field' (how's that for a metaphor?) – in other words, that everyone has the essential knowledge required to deliver a speech with impact, before we teach them the 'difference that makes the difference' material.

So, in this chapter, we will be referencing certain areas, making them practicable at home, whilst always bearing in mind that delivery skills are best when they are practised in the moment, face-to-face. We shall be looking at a system devised for the delivery elements needed to engage an audience on a world class level, and it is:

Mindset **A**ctions **S**tance **T**onality **E**ye contact **R**ehearsal Be **Y**ourself

This is not to say that if you use these techniques with proficiency you will be a delivery master. Mastery is both an overused – and a misused – term. Rather, the suggestion is that mastery is achieved as a result of a lifetime's application.

What the acronym *does* claim is that *if* you can use these techniques until you are habitual, natural and authentic, you will be on the right road to achieving delivery mastery in the future.

While we're on the subject of claims, we would also suggest that the vast majority of professional speakers have reached the 'good' stage, without necessarily progressing past that.

The reasons for this are:

- There is a lack of self-awareness with most speakers we see (Chapter 2: Mindset); as a result, the quality is compromised which in turn eats away at the self-belief.

- There is a lack of craft in their storytelling skills (Chapter 5).

- And lastly, when delivering on stage, the suggestion is that the majority of speakers are not putting enough thought into their impact upon their audience (Chapter 4: The Audience and this chapter).

So, to address the first point, how do we know that there is a lack of awareness?

The reason we suggest this is that we often see speakers who are preaching one thing and doing another. For example, as witnessed the other day at a conference in Chile for one of the 'big four' consulting firms, the keynote speaker had a CV as long as his arm, and was exhorting the audience to make 'death by PowerPoint' a thing of the past. In other words, he was drawing attention to the age-old trap of many speakers, who cram their slides with masses of data and then 'talk to the slides' rather than to the audience.

What did he then do? Precisely that! He had some points to talk through and addressed his whole message not to the audience but to the slides!

The second point made at the start of this chapter was concerning the lack of craft in the storytelling. This is also remarkable; supposed professional speakers really ought to know what they are doing when it comes to the structure of storytelling, but sadly, this often disappears 'in the moment'.

The third and last point about not putting oneself into one's audience's shoes is manifestly evident in the two points we have just looked at.

But it's more than that; the *priority* of *transposing* – or putting yourself into someone else's position – is in the main the biggest blind spot of the public speaker. With this lack comes the abiding focus on *self* rather than the audience, the lack of focus, the lack of authenticity and ultimately the lack of desirable results as an outcome of all these factors.

Bridging the gap from good to great, then, is all about a raised level of awareness about current strengths and potential flaws that can undermine those strengths. Subject matter expertise is not enough to get the job done.

As an example, a fellow professional and colleague spent an interesting week with a group of senior executives from a global bank recently, where the focus was on tips and techniques for handling pressure, influence, impact and leadership.

What is consistently striking about working with the upper echelons from any organisation is how impressive individuals become when forged in the fire of tough negotiation, selling and leading from the front under pressure. The consensus amongst most professionals working in the field of skills development is that we always learn as much as we teach.

What is really challenging, however, is how rarely this expertise, knowledge and business acumen is translated into *charismatic communication*.

On the final day, he charged the group with preparing a two-minute talk on what they had learnt and what they were going to use after the workshop. Without exception, yes, the experience shone through with each mini presentation, and whilst a few nuggets of pure managerial gold were shared, none of the individuals stood out as being charismatic.

A key point to remember then, as mentioned in Chapter 1, is that charisma, whilst more geared naturally towards some than others, is a skill that can be learnt.

Let's look in a little more detail into the ingredients that comprise this 'ingredient X' and take the elements of delivery **M A S T E R Y** one at a time.

Mindset – the difference that makes the difference.

We have talked in some detail about the mindset elements needed for a resourceful and progressive approach to resilience and self-development. The mindset element here is specifically for on-stage preparation.

Self-talk

As discussed in Chapter 2, we all talk to ourselves; together with seeing internal images (which we will come on to), it's the way we think.

The question here is: when you are in a potentially high-stakes situation and you may be feeling the pressure, what is it that you do/say to yourself? Are you aware of what you are saying to yourself, or is it just… happening?

A popular opinion is that it is the latter – it just happens. It's as if we have a totally independent mischief-maker inside our heads, rather like the devil v the angel, perched upon our shoulders, whispering nasty nothings into our ears.

Self-talk, or self-affirmation, is generally a belief, a feeling of certainty, which then drives the chain reaction we have just spoken of, so as a result, it's really important to make sure your self-talk is in *positive* affirmation rather than negative.

Some examples might be: 'I can do this', or 'I'm going to smash this', or 'I'm going to enjoy this', rather than the autopilot 'I'm terrified' or 'I can't do this.'

See the difference? So the answer is actually very simple and will have tangible results upon your mindset and consequently your performance.

A strong recommendation is that you make a note in your **rejoice, reframe, refine** journal, to make some consciously empowering self-affirmations, every time you are in a potentially pressured situation.

The more you can raise awareness, as mentioned in Chapter 2, the more control you have over your performance and results. The key is to be consistent with this new strategy until it has become habitual.

Body talk

You may know those times when you have to make a speech or give a presentation and your preparation is all going wrong. It's a bit like 'brain to body – time to feel anxious and scared' and the body says, 'no problem brain – here you are!' and manifests nervous, low-powered posture, which, sure enough, creates feelings of nerves and worry. This chain reaction happens without conscious thought, but it is undeniable that the link between our body language and how we feel is inextricably linked. In other words, in order to feel a certain way, you have to *use your body* in a certain way.

Why is this fantastic news?

If you already use your body language to create emotional states unconsciously, you can use your body language on purpose to create feelings of emotional certainty, energy and confidence. It's just a matter of switching off your automatic pilot, asking yourself the question: How do I need to feel in this situation? and then adopting the appropriate posture.

By the way, facial expressions come into this and a smile is one of the fastest ways to change your, and others', emotional state; the problem is, when we're under stress, the last thing we think of doing is smiling!

So remember, the fastest way to feel good in a challenging situation is to consciously choose an empowering posture. That's the *internal* secret sauce taken care of – and it really does work.

If you are one of those who enjoy scientific proof, I would recommend you to watch Amy Cuddy's brilliant TED talk about body language and how it can affect our body chemistry – either for better or for worse. Her strapline for her talk is 'fake it until you become it'; the alteration of the original 'make' from the well-known phrase to 'become' is all about the change in our chemistry and the emotions, behaviour and results that ensue. She talks about the two main hormones that control our confidence (testosterone) and conversely our stress levels (cortisol).

In very abbreviated form, her talk explores the research she has carried out at Harvard University, where she divided a group of participants in two and asked one half to adopt what she calls 'high power poses' for two minutes and the other half to adopt 'low power poses' for two minutes. She then measured their testosterone and cortisol levels using a saliva test. The results were conclusive: the 'high power pose' students had both considerably higher testosterone (confidence) levels, *plus* considerably lower cortisol (stress) levels after the two-minute exercise. The 'low power pose' students, on the other hand, had demonstrably lower testosterone (confidence) levels and demonstrably higher cortisol (stress) levels.

What do these findings tell us?

Essentially, our body language drives either low stress and high confidence or high stress and low confidence, depending upon which body language postures we adopt. Your body language, or physiology, remains the quickest way to change your emotional state – either consciously for the better or unconsciously for the worse.

Once again, as with the self-talk, the big challenge comes when our autopilot is switched on and we allow our body language to control our emotions, along with our unresourceful self-talk.

Body language comes in different forms: there are our facial expressions, our posture, our breathing and our movement – and all of these are critical, both for altering our emotional state for the better and for engaging our audience at the same time.

Facial expressions

It always provokes a smile in our 1:1 speaker coaching sessions when the presenter delivers his or her speech with a deadpan serious face.

That's not to say that they are being laughed at – far from it. It is more the recognition of two of the big obstacles that get in the way of any speaker's success:

1. The autopilot – when we feel pressure, what's the last thing we feel like doing? You've guessed it – smiling!

2. Culture. Many of our clients work in high-powered positions either at the head of – or at least the neck of – huge corporations. As such, they spend their lives buried in corporate culture, which in most cases is deadly serious…'we work for a living here, fun isn't allowed'. As a result, people become conditioned to adopting serious faces for serious topics.

Now please don't think that the important work that our clients do is being trivialised. It's not that.

You remember the quote, supposedly by Dr Seuss: *'Why do we try to fit in when we were born to stand out?'*

The key to a great speech isn't the content, it's the *speaker*. As a result, the two reasons above – the automatic response to pressure, which causes so many people to try and look as anodyne as possible, or 'fit in', plus the conditioned 'corporate' facial expressions – need to be addressed if you are going to come across as authentic, relaxed and passionate.

Make a note in your journal to consciously remember to smile!

Just to be clear: we are not advocating grinning like an idiot all the way through your important corporate message; a smile is a powerful tool and needs to be used sparingly. A smile sends a very important signal: that you are both enjoying yourself *and* that you are making recognition to your audience that this is a *human* interaction, rather than mere data transfer.

The last point here is a question: with the exception of the London underground, what happens when you smile at someone?

Breathing

Once again, the breathing element is total common sense here. We all know that deep breathing is a relaxing strategy. It oxygenates the blood, as well as relaxing our parasympathetic nervous system. From a speaking perspective, it also gives us a powerful support for our voice – more on that later in the chapter.

The question to you is this: it may be common sense to breathe deeply when the pressure is on, but is it common practice?

But why not?

We don't follow common sense because our fears and inhibitions cause us to protect rather than perform. However, once again, the answer is simple if not simplistic. It's all about making a *conscious* choice to breathe deeply before entering a potentially stressful situation, such as delivering an important speech to a large audience.

Movement

Movement is both a delivery technique and a mindset strategy. I will come on to the delivery side when we reach the **A**ctions section of delivery **M A S T E R Y.**

As far as the mindset element of movement is concerned, consider the taking of exercise. Whether you go to the gym, or play a sport, or go for long walks or cycle rides, the effects upon our bodies and minds are the same. As well as heightened energy, neurotransmitters such as the endorphins dopamine and serotonin are released into the body, which are well recognised as mood enhancers. So it's all good news – you feel energised and you also feel good.

The related benefits to the public speaker are clear. Now the suggestion is not that you go for a run immediately before delivering your speech, literally leaving the cross-trainer to run on stage. However, a great idea and habit to get into is a series of stretches (if you are in the wings by the side of the stage and out of the audience's eyeline, or conversely, if you are outside the side doors to the auditorium, awaiting the call to the stage) to loosen the muscles and get the blood flowing.

You can also make sure that you have a little walk to get on to the platform – not enough to look like a show-off (no one likes a show-off) from the back of the auditorium, but just enough to use the few steps to energise yourself, so you can 'hit the ground running'.

Note: this, like everything else, needs practice to look natural and not rehearsed.

So once again, remember that conscious plans to use movement – just like the other techniques cited here in order to promote and maintain a resourceful state – are the only things that will make this happen, so the advice is to make another note in your journal to that effect.

Visualisation

The last mindset element is an integral part of our everyday life: the power of visualisation. Once again, you will not be surprised to read that visualisation is not rocket science, it is actually a very simple process and the process by which we think moment to moment.

Just try this for a second: close your eyes and imagine your front door.

Done it? You have successfully visualised!

Now whilst visualisation has become a well-respected and proven peak performance strategy in sports for some time, it has also received growing recognition in some business sectors.

The idea behind visualisation – seeing a successful outcome in your mind's eye before it even happens – is that the brain cannot tell the difference between what is real and what is vividly imagined. In other words, if you imagine a successful outcome really clearly and vividly in your mind, the brain thinks it is really happening, so when you actually get to go through the experience itself, the brain has made sure that as much potential as possible is showing up because it knows what success looks like already.

Visualising as a technique has popularly been used as a psychological advantage in the world of sport for many years now. In recent years, it has been used more and more in other fields, for the simple reason that if you visualise a successful outcome, far more of that potential will show up. Human beings imagine things in pictures. The movies we play in our minds have a gigantic effect on how we feel about something. The challenge is that most of us play our inner movies a) unconsciously and b) the wrong way round. In other words, we play the disaster movie in our heads – all the things that *can* go wrong *are* going wrong!

So there is a simple solution and that is to *consciously* get into the habit of playing helpful movies in our minds of us succeeding. There is huge evidence to suggest that living the future now or 'acting as if' is a very powerful means of engaging the brain and setting the RAS towards your goal and achieving it.

Whatever your goal may be, the key here is to visualise your achieving it so clearly that it appears real. With clear imagination and visualisation come the same beliefs, emotions and behaviours that will drive you towards the outcome you want.

Of course, there is nothing as important or as effective as real practice. It's not enough to know the steps – you have to take action, as mentioned in Chapter 1.

Actions

The second element in the delivery **M A S T E R Y** programme is the **A**ctions that will make the biggest positive impact upon your audience.

Actions fall into two categories: movement and gestures.

Movement

Opinion is sharply divided when it comes to moving when delivering a speech on a platform in front of an audience. Some say, yes, for goodness' sake move around or you'll look stiff and unnatural; for others, movement on stage is seen as a near heresy.

So what are the do's and don'ts with regard to movement on stage?

Statistics tell us that an audience will relate best to a speaker who is comfortable in his or her skin – someone who is clearly at ease with themselves in what most people see as a hostile and challenging environment.

As a result, it could be said that the application of movement as a strategy is very much a 'horses for courses' approach. The most important thing to remember, as we have – by now often – said throughout this book, is that the audience comes first.

If you are delivering a high-energy speech about a topic that requires urgency and passion, then you might want to consider more movement as a strategy. If you are speaking about a more reflective, considered topic, then less movement might be your approach.

Most importantly, there are three absolutely *unbreakable* ground rules:

1. ALWAYS *have a reason for moving*

In other words, always move *with* purpose and *on* purpose.

The reason for this is that as far as your audience is concerned, anything that *can* be a distraction *will* be a distraction. If you are just wandering about (because you tell yourself that you can think better that way, or because it's more comfortable for you to move rather than to stand still) with no purpose, the audience will wonder why. This will take the focus away from your subject – even if it is brilliant – and all people will remember is the pacing up and down.

So, in practical terms, what does 'moving with a reason' actually look like?

In general, you have various 'reasons' for moving, which go as follows:

If in front of a big audience, you may want to move to address one side, then move to the middle, then move to other side.

If you are taking questions, or facilitating an activity, then there are generally lots of opportunities for moving: stepping towards a questioner for example, or pointing out various members of the audience depending upon your activity. Again, depending on the activity, there may even be an opportunity to move *amongst* your audience.

Flipcharts provide a great opportunity for moving, as do certain features on slides.

Lastly – and this involves movement to an extent – always move forward and centrally to the edge of the stage when you are about to deliver a key message.

2. *With reference to the above point, try not to move when you are delivering a key point.* The audience needs to understand that you mean what you say and there should be no distraction while you do this.

3. *PLAN!*

    It doesn't ring true when people reluctantly come to our speaker coaching sessions using the rationale: 'I'm much better when I just get up and do it on the day.'

    Every time this happens, a nod should be given to the fact that spontaneity is a great commodity, but a big fat shake of the head to the claim that planning curtails the ability to be spontaneous.

    Planning will not curtail spontaneity and a more forthright explanation is often that people use this as an excuse.

In the acting world, 'blocking' is the process where the director, together with his company, will work out what the best moves are for each scene; in other words, who moves when, and on which line. The reason for this is clear: if actors moved about aimlessly, there would be no form or purpose or direction to any scene. The blocking process makes sure that movement and placement are positioned in the best way possible to achieve coherence and the maximum dramatic effect.

It is only after this is arranged that the actors can start to rehearse and to express their characters and make them their own. The blocking, like a skeleton, supports everything around it, and without the skeleton the body collapses in a heap.

It's the same with your speech. If you plan, or block, where you are going to move, depending upon the nature of the speech and the size and nature of the audience, you can put your mind at rest because you have worked out a physical structure that supports your material and gives you the maximum dramatic effect when you come to deliver your speech. Once you have worked out where and how to move, and when, and you have practised these moves, you have hard-wired these, so you are already going to look polished and you can forget about them.

The delivery skills, structure, stories etc. haven't even happened yet, so the planning of your movement shouldn't interfere in any way with your spontaneity of delivery.

Gestures

The second part of the **A**ctions element is where much of the alchemy of the speaker comes into play. And here's why.

Whilst our ape ancestors have been walking the planet for millions of years, our direct human ancestors have existed for an approximate 200,000 years. We started to talk an estimated 100,000 years ago, which means that we communicated just through body language for as long as we have used speech since!

Various studies in the last 40 years have broken down the elements of communication into three distinct parts: words (the message itself), voice and vocal tone, and lastly body language. The figures are quite startling. According to extensive research carried out largely in the 70s and 80s, the impact of the words in face-to-face communication has been estimated at a staggering 7%.

This means that your content – *what* you say – has a minimal impact on your audience compared to the 93% communicated through vocal tone and body language. Of this, an approximate 55% was attributed to body language.

Whilst the statistics are a pointer and may vary according to the situation, the fact remains that over half of the impact in our face-to-face communication comes from the elements that comprise body language.

As you look at the image below, you will see how the brain sees body language. By far and away the most impactful element comes from the hands, which means that your gestures are the conductors of the physical orchestra and will attract the attention of the audience, whether by accident or by design.

In a similar way to the blocking elements of movement described above, the gestures you use can also be designed and planned, depending on various factors.

The size of your audience

For a small audience of say 50 people, you may want to make your gestures 'fit' into the space and the audience size, so try to think of a space the size of a football as the hand gesture arena.

For a medium sized audience of 100-200 people, the same maxim applies, but try to make your gestures slightly bigger so everyone can see them and you are neither underplaying nor overplaying your 'hand'.

Lastly, for the larger audiences of 250-10,000, the sky is the limit. You can use your whole wingspan.

Size doesn't always represent the only important factor here. Try and *think of your audience* and the type of people you are speaking to. For a more conservative audience, perhaps of senior leaders or an audience from the more cerebral professions such as accounting, banking and insurance for example, you might want to think of tailoring your gestures in a more 'conservative' way.

To bring your speech to life

As well as tailoring your gestures, you can also use your hands as a visual representation of a verbal message. In other words, when you use your gestures on purpose and with purpose, you are combining the voice and body language impact into the 93% that we mentioned earlier.

Here are some examples:

- Itemising – If you count the items you are describing on your fingers, it helps the audience's comprehension by giving their brains two sense receptors instead of just one.

- Descriptive – By using your hands in a descriptive way to tell your story physically as you describe it vocally, you make your speech much easier to understand than if you were just speaking. It's a *visual reinforcement* of a vocal message.

- Lastly, you can use certain gestures to convey the mood and the intensity of your speech. These use universal, globally recognised body postures with gestures to convey meaning.

For example, if you are looking to convey calm in a potentially inflammatory scenario, make a controversial point, or break bad news, what's the classically accepted gesture? Try standing with your hands flat and your palms upwards – it is totally non-threatening and sends a powerful message of appeasement. You might consider slightly raised eyebrows at the same time.

If you are looking to consider either a point you have made or a question from your audience, the aim is to send a message that clearly states that you are seriously considering the point at issue in a logical way. Common sense once again dictates that you fold one arm across your front which supports the other whose hand is 'propping up' your chin, as if in thought.

A third '*with* purpose and *on* purpose' gesture/body position that has great impact is when you are looking to make that important point you have stepped forward and are facing the audience. As you make your point, hold your hands about body width apart, with your hands flat and your palms downwards. This conveys trustworthiness and, in a way, is saying 'I'm being truthful and I have nothing to hide – I really mean this.'

Remember, body language has more impact than *what* you say or *how* you say it. Your rehearsed gestures, facial expressions and posture will represent the difference that makes the difference.

Rest positions

One of the biggest giveaways to a speaker's comfort level and professionalism is what they do with their hands when they are speaking, when they are gesturing, and critically, what they do when they are *not* gesturing.

As a result, one of the most often asked questions people ask is: 'What should I do with my hands when I'm not using them?' The answer is not set in stone, there are various options available. The key is to both *look* and *feel* comfortable with your hands.

Option 1 – hands at your sides (recommended)

If you think about this, this is our natural stance as human beings. If we relax, our hands hang at our sides in a natural, comfortable way. We are not fidgeting, crossing anything or being 'tricksy' – we are just standing in our natural human position.

This is important because a natural, relaxed stance sends a powerful message that we have nothing to hide – that this is us. As you stand with your hands at your sides, you can gesture when required with either or both hands, and critically, you don't have to worry whether your hands are being a distraction.

There is a challenge with this 'resting position'. As children, we learn from adults, who in turn have learned that the world is a scary place and that we need to protect ourselves. As a result, if you look at *any* group of adults in *any* kind of interaction, whether networking or at a social gathering, you will see immediately that the custom is to cross everything wherever possible – both arms and legs, the classic subconscious protective gesture.

If you look at a group pose for a photograph, you can be certain that very few – if any – people will stand with their hands by their sides. Why? Because it is strangely vulnerable, there is no 'protection'.

It is no accident that actors in training spend several months learning how to stand with their hands by their sides. Why? Because it is only when you are vulnerable that your authenticity can be seen. Actors seek to 'be truthful' and they can only do this through authenticity. It's the same when you speak with your hands at your sides.

Lastly, because it has a feeling of vulnerability about it, it is also unequalled in communicating confidence. As a result, because so few people do it – even professional speakers – it's a key differentiator.

Option 2 – the 'waiter'

You may have seen how waiters often stand, with one arm by their side and the other in front of their body at right angles, often with a napkin draped over it. This is another rest position you might want to try. It's not as taxing as standing with both hands by your sides – there is some 'protection'. It's also quite handy if you have a clicker. You can click with the hand by your side and gesture with the other.

As mentioned, this is all about making it easy for you and not distracting the audience.

Option 3 – hands bent at right angles with the hands meeting in the middle with a variety of options:

- The steeple – both hands pointed towards your audience, fingertips together

- The overlay – one hand laid *lightly* over the other

- The gap – the hands held naturally towards the audience, six to nine inches apart

All of these work, are interchangeable (so you can mix them up as required) and are highly practical ways of having your hands there when you need them, without distracting your audience. It's just a matter of trying them out to see how they feel – get someone to give you feedback as to how each looks on you.

The 'no-no's'

In the same way that some rest positions are effective means of communicating comfort and ease of gesturing, others can communicate acute discomfort and are to be avoided at all costs.

Arms crossed

This is a well-recognised sign of a barrier: it communicates to an audience that you don't want to be there, you don't want to 'let them in', or that you have made up your mind and won't budge. So, uncomfortable or obstinate – neither is great.

Arms behind back

Given that your hands are such potent 'weapons' of communication when used properly, why on earth would you 'tie' them behind your back? This is often used when people genuinely don't know what to do with their hands. They've seen other people do it, so why not do it themselves? It can also look either teacher-like or slightly aggressive.

The football 'wall'

Probably the most common of them all and the most defensive. If you are a football fanatic, this is for you! What do the defenders in a 'wall' do, just before a free kick? They cover their groin, quite sensibly.

In a speaking scenario please try and avoid this, for two reasons: firstly, it gives the impression that you are about as uncomfortable as you can possibly be; secondly, people follow the hands, remember? If you want people to look at your groin, this is what you do!

Clasping the hands

Whereas the steeple and the overlay are great examples of the hands together and represent a great way of both 'resting' and using the hands when needed, the hand clasp is not recommended because there is a tendency under pressure to 'wring' them, which completely undermines any attempt to look at ease. The other possibility is to clasp them so tightly that all the audience will see is the classic set of 'white knuckles'. Not a great idea.

Stance

Let's have a look at the significant area of influencing others comprised by posture. Posture is best described as the way we sit or stand. The *external* part is about creating the impression of yourself you want in others.

Have you ever asked yourself what it is about someone that gives them a certain 'something'? You may not even know them to speak to. The chances are that in most situations the strongest impression will be made through the body language. We are impressed by the way certain people hold themselves, either sitting or standing, just as we make character assassinations of people who slouch, slump or habitually adopt a less than resourceful posture. As with good public speakers, this *never* happens by accident – ever! Good posture and stance come from hard work, discipline and self-awareness. It's about remembering that you cannot *not* communicate.

Whether you like it or not, you are sending out signals on a subconscious – and often on a conscious – level about how you are feeling about yourself, or about others, or both, through your posture and stance, together with the gestures and facial expressions that we have mentioned earlier.

So, rule of thumb: sit up straight as often as you can, in order to form a habit of good posture; as mentioned, this takes approximately two months of consistent practice to embed.

Try not to use the back of your chair. It'll do wonders for your lower back and will eventually become habitual, so long as you make it a focus. Remember, you are sending *internal* signals of strength and wellbeing by doing this, as well as letting the world know that your self-image demands a good strong posture.

If you communicate face-to-face on a regular basis, remember that, if seated, leaning in towards them with an open posture (i.e. no folded arms) sends a very positive message of confidence and amity. If you want others to relax, you can also lead others into a more relaxed state by leaning back in your chair on occasion. There is no right or wrong posture, or stance, as long as you adopt it *with* purpose and *on* purpose.

The heart follows the feet

Another important thing to remember is that 'the heart follows the feet'. What is meant by this is a very simple tip which will tell your audience that you *want to be there*. Just make sure that your feet are pointing towards your audience as opposed to away from them or off to the side.

Once again, this isn't the kind of thing we consciously notice but, nonetheless, it sends a powerful subconscious signal to your audience that you are comfortable with the experience.

Crossed legs

In a similar way, self-awareness plays its part when you are looking to convey confidence to your audience. A common mistake people make is that they will cross their legs – in a very similar way that they will fold their arms – because it feels more comfortable in a pressurised situation. However, as we know with the folded arms, the signal we send is unmistakably that we do not want to be there!

The solution is simple: switch off your autopilot and rehearse using open body language with a strong open stance. It may feel exposing to begin with but as with all new habits, it will become second nature very quickly.

Preferred weight

In exactly the same way, we will shift our weight from an even keel to one side because it just feels more comfortable for us when we feel pressure. Just remember, what may feel comfortable for you will send very clear signals to the audience that you aren't happy where you are.

Remember, anything that *can* be a distraction *will* be a distraction so remember to make your body language as difficult to misinterpret as possible. Balanced, open and even distribution does the trick.

It isn't easy because you have to remain vigilant, especially when you have spent your life to date *unconsciously* replicating body language consonant with the emotional state your brain is telling you to feel.

Tone

The next element of the delivery **M A S T E R Y** formula is **T**one. As you will remember, vocal delivery comprises 38% of the impact in face-to-face communication, so this is a very important element to master.

There is a lot to recognise here that can't be explored in a book and needs practical experience and, as with everything else explained here, you have the option to visit our website for video tutorials, as well as experience the workshops themselves for more insights and that all-important practice. In the meantime, here are a couple of vocal pointers.

Breathing

Our most vital requirement as a communicator is breath – outside of the obvious need for oxygen, that is!

It makes total sense that regular deep breaths will support the voice. In the same way as a singer, if you have a deep lungful of oxygen as you start a sentence, you will have enough breath to start it strongly and, just as important, to *finish* it strongly as well. A great tip for best practice is to go on to YouTube and watch a professional classical singer in action.

Once again, it's not rocket science but it does take practice, especially as when we are under pressure, the breath, if unmonitored, tends to be shallow and is an enemy rather than an ally to the communicator.

As a speaker, breath allows us to use our voice in the following ways:

Pace

The first element to remember is that when people feel pressure when communicating, the most common mistake they make is to speed up. The rationale is clear and, once again, the autopilot is the enemy of excellence.

Without conscious thought, our brain goes into fight or flight mode when we are experiencing a stressful situation and, as a result, the flight impulse sends a very urgent message to our limbic centre to speed up. Now our conscious, rational brain knows that this is not going to help, but the emotional brain will always win unless we are disciplined and practise a conscious process of slowing down.

At the other end of the spectrum, the opposite of going too fast is… the pause.

Pause

What does a good pause do? The answer comes in several parts:

- It creates a space for the audience to reflect on the point made

- It creates drama – a pause leaves speculation in the air

- It leaves the audience in no doubt that you are making a point that you believe in deeply

- Lastly – and here's the biggest point – if you leave a pause, you are sending a very powerful signal to the audience that you are quite comfortable in your own skin

The reason for this is that human beings have an almost pathological fear of silence – isn't that true? The challenge with pausing is of course that it's hard to do – it flies in the face of self-preservation. At some level, your brain is saying, 'If I stop speaking, they're going to stop listening to what I'm saying and will start looking at ME!'

This is one of the main reasons why so much focus has been given to mindset in this book. The skills required to stand up and 'wow' an audience take practice and honing, but they will only be practised and honed if the speaker *genuinely* wants to be there, if the speaker allows himself or herself to get into the right positive frame of mind to do so in the first place.

Understanding

Our voice creates understanding. Clarity is an elusive quality when communicating because there are various factors that can get in the way: lack of preparation and rehearsal can cause us to garble, nerves can cause us to clam up, but a few deep breaths, as we know well, will calm us. The challenge is that slow deep breathing is not something we think of under pressure because we are too busy feeling… pressured!

The solution? To be understood, practise and prepare until you know that you can communicate the message you want to communicate in the way that you want to communicate it. But take a few breaths first as it will calm you and help you to focus on the job in hand – to get your message across.

Light and shade

Light and shade, or modulation as it's commonly known, is a means by which to create distinctions in your narrative that will differentiate you in a powerful way. I want you to think about the very worst presentations and speeches that you may have heard. The generally accepted 'no-no' that really disengages an audience is the monotone delivery. Everyone knows consciously that speaking in a monotone is not going to engage *anyone*.

So why does it happen? And happen so often?

Once again, speaking in public, whether presenting or delivering a speech, is a high-stakes situation and the human autopilot, if not closely regulated, will look to make you as anonymous as possible. As a result, unless well-rehearsed, people tend to speak quietly and as 'unremarkably' as possible – whether they intend to do so or not – because it's a self-preservation technique.

The solution? Take a moment to recognise your natural voice when you are chatting with your family or friends. That's what you need to be doing when you are delivering a presentation or speech. People get this so wrong – they feel that because they are on stage or making an official speech they need to 'formalise' what they are saying.

Remember, *nothing* will create engagement with your audience as fast as you being authentically you, and that means the natural conversational you. Imagine that you are chatting to friends – and you will be.

Support

Yet again, our unconscious state is reactive. When we feel the pressure of a situation, such as walking on to a stage, the autopilot reaction is to breathe shallowly and in the chest rather than from the diaphragm. Deep, resonant diaphragmatic breathing will centre you, will allow you to support your voice with power and to 'throw' your sound so that it carries. If ever you have received feedback that people can't hear you, or that you speak too quietly, it's all about breath control.

The answer? Babies teach us how to breathe. The next chance you get, watch a baby as it sleeps. It won't be breathing from its chest but from its belly. Practise diaphragmatic breathing by placing your hand on your abdomen and consciously breathing as deeply as you can. As with every other exercise here, practice makes perfect. Test the theory by breathing shallowly from your chest and delivering a line of your speech or presentation, then try the new technique and see the difference.

Emphasis

Let's look at an example.

The phrase 'I never said I hugged your wife' comprises seven words, for example. Try speaking the whole sentence, putting the vocal emphasis on the first word:

'I never said I hugged your wife.' Meaning? I didn't, but someone else did.

Next: *'I **never** said I hugged your wife.'* Meaning? Denial!

Next: *'I never **said** I hugged your wife.'* Meaning? I may have implied it!

Next: *'I never said **I** hugged your wife.'* Meaning? Someone else hugged her!

Next: *'I never said I **hugged** your wife.'* Meaning? Unprintable!

Next: *'I never said I hugged **your** wife.'* Meaning? I hugged someone else's wife!

Lastly: *'I never said I hugged your **wife**.'* Meaning? I hugged the dog!

A seven word sentence – seven different meanings.

And the point? You create meaning with vocal emphasis – plain and simple.

So in practical terms, how do you make this work? The suggestion here is all in the planning and the rehearsal. Have a think about which points in your speech are the most important and then practise pointing these with a combination of vocal emphasis and then 'turbocharging' your point with a pause. As with everything else to do with delivery, the more you practise and rehearse, the more comfortable you will be in your skin, and therefore the better you will be.

Eye contact

There are various schools of thought, but if you think about a communication from the audience's perspective – whether in a team meeting or a larger scenario – what they really want is to *have a connection* with the speaker.

The challenge with most communication of this sort is that it comes from the perspective of the speaker: 'what *I* want to tell you, what *I* want you to hear'.

With a change in perspective, when the speaker starts to think about what he or she wants the receiver to *think, feel and do differently* as a result of the communication, the intent becomes clearer and eye contact hits a more focused level.

Most communicators will engage in what I like to call the 'machine-gun' approach, where they will scan their audience from side to side. They may even look at individuals randomly for a second or two before moving on. The effect this has is that the speaker is addressing a group of people but still with the intent of speaking to a group.

The magic happens when the speaker uses a technique which involves one person for one thought. As the speaker communicates each thought, he or she looks at one person and nowhere else – not up or down or side to side, just laser-like eye contact on that one individual for the duration of the thought or sentence. In time terms, this is normally five seconds or so.

Having done the hard work of making the eye contact, make sure that you stay on that individual until you have finished the thought. If you move your eyes before you have finished, the message is lost because it will feel to the receiver that you don't really mean what you say. Having delivered your message to that individual, you then move to someone else.

Three things:

1. Make sure that you move your eye contact randomly. If you start on one person and then just move along the line, the message to the audience is that you will get to them eventually, but in sequence. The individuals at the end of the line will know that they have a little time before you get to them and the chances are that they will switch off.

2. Make sure that you remember the extremities of the space. Traditionally, the people to both sides don't receive much 'love' because the speaker will normally focus on a 30 degree angle in front of him or her.

3. Remember, you are 'educating' your audience. As a result, try to ensure that you maintain this technique even if the person you are addressing looks away. Give it a try; the good thing about this technique is that you can practise it at any time you are talking to a group of three or more people. Just be aware that this is, at its finest, an art form. You will not believe the difference it will make to the impact you have on any audience with this technique because the intent is clear: you want to have an individual connection in a group setting.

Finally, just remember that anything worth having takes work.

Rehearse

When I think back to my acting days, if anyone suggested the idea of putting on a play without rehearsals, he or she would be laughed out of the theatre. It's inconceivable to think of not rehearsing a play and it should be the same with your speech.

Barack Obama, widely recognised as one of the world's great orators, looks natural and at ease when he speaks. Do you think he practises? You'd better believe he does. He hasn't reached the level he has reached through natural ability alone.

The old adage – so old in fact that opinion is now divided as to who originally said it – 'the more I practise, the luckier I get' (it was a golfer – some say Palmer, others say Player) holds true in every area where people look to excel. And public speaking is no exception.

The rehearsal process has several benefits:

- Firstly, it ensures the smooth running of your speech by ironing out any 'clunkiness' or lack of cohesion, both in subject matter and delivery

- Rehearsal allows you to feel more practised, therefore more professional and therefore more confident

- Rehearsal allows you to get the timing of your speech right. There are few things worse than running over – it makes you look unprofessional and there is no worse feeling as a speaker to run out of things to say before your slot is 'done'

- Rehearsing reminds me of the old Martini advertisements – you can rehearse any time, any place, anywhere. There's no excuse for not doing it

Yourself

'Authenticity is a collection of choices that we have to make every day. It's about the choice to show up and be real. The choice to be honest. The choice to let our true selves be seen.'

Brené Brown

The last element in the M A S T E R Y chain is **Yourself**.

One of the most enjoyable 'hats' that I wear in my job as a speaker is 1:1 speaker coaching for individuals.

I was giving some coaching to a very senior executive who was preparing to go before the board of a public company for an amazing job opportunity. He was talking with great excitement about the fact that he had to be 'on his game' and to 'know his stuff'. Both good points and very important to make sure of, but as far as getting the job was concerned, he was focusing exclusively on the rational drivers of his audience.

As we have discussed, people buy into things emotionally. They may justify this decision rationally, but the limbic, or emotional, brain will respond to emotional rather than rational stimulus.

As also mentioned, it's important that the rational material is in there. In other words, 'knowing your stuff' will get you on to the short list, along with other candidates who also know their stuff; but what will get you the job, or the contract, or the engagement, is how people buy into *you*.

You are your biggest asset. It's not the slides (rational) or the material (rational) that you discuss that makes the difference; it's how you present yourself, how you engage with your audience and how much they trust you and empathise with you at the end of your 'slot' (emotional).

What's more, people will evaluate you both consciously and subconsciously – it's all going on in a face-to-face intervention. Remember, we communicated for 100,000 years on this planet before we learned to speak, so an instinctive understanding and communication is going on all the time through our unspoken body language.

Try and think of it this way: you cannot *not* communicate. And your body language doesn't lie. People will be picking up your 'truth' whether you like it or not.

And the answer? How do you present 'yourself', the *true* you, the *essence* of you, to your audience and customers? It's not easy, after all, because we know that authenticity is OK when there's no pressure, but in a high-stakes situation such as a speech or a presentation, our resident inner critic is whispering nasty nothings into our ear and our real self tends to run and hide, leaving just our 'emergency self' behind – i.e. stiff, self-conscious and exposed.

At the risk of sounding smug, I believe from my experience that the answer lies in the culmination of the other elements in M A S T E R Y, with particular reference to the M – Mindset and the R –

Rehearsal. The more practised you are, the more Rehearsed you are, the more natural and comfortable will be your Actions, Stance, Tone and Eye contact and consequently the easier the application of the most resourceful Mindset.

Don't take yourself too seriously

Lastly, on the subject of yourself, a footnote. Try and remember that in the grand scheme of things the speech you are about to make really isn't the 'be all and end all'. It's a speech, that's all. It's your job to communicate a message as best you can, but no one's going to die.

The more you carry this thought into bigger and bigger stages and higher and higher stakes, the more it will make sense to you. It made the difference as I was about to walk out on stage in front of my first audience of 5,000 people and if you remember to use it, it will help you too.

Summary

A packed chapter, the attention has been upon the following:

- **Mindset**

Specifically: delivery or communication mindset, comprising the various techniques that will help you both before you walk into the limelight and then while you are in the heat of battle as well

- **Actions**

Specifically: gestures and movement – the do's and don'ts

- **Stance**

Some key distinctions around your stance and posture

- **Tone**

Your vocal delivery tips, comprising the PULSE – Pace, Understanding, Light and shade, Support and Emphasis

- *E*ye **contact**

Arguably the most important element, including a tip to engage everyone in the audience

- *R*ehearsal

It doesn't matter how well you prepare, if you don't rehearse, you're setting yourself up for a big challenge

- *Yourself*

Lastly, some ideas around authenticity – if you can feel like you're chatting to friends, you're halfway there

CHAPTER 7
THE PROMOTION

*'People don't buy what you do,
they buy why you do it.'*

Simon Sinek

In this chapter we will be looking at the following:

- Some different ways in which you can turn your knowledge into easily accessible and valuable products and services for your target market

- The way to blend your content for both face-to-face and online interventions

- Promotion ideas

So far, we have looked at the following areas:

The Opportunity

A methodology of clarifying your purpose and objectives.

The Mindset

Nothing works without resilience. Clarity of focus and some clear steps to maintaining mental toughness and self-development.

The Content

A methodology for creating catchy, memorable content that is easy to understand, to teach and to use. In addition, some stagecraft techniques to engage your audience and give your delivery huge impact.

The Audience

A six step planning structure from your audience's perspective.

The Story

An understanding of the power of the story and how it can elevate a speaker from good to flipping brilliant!

The Mastery

The critical steps to building world-class speaker skills that will inspire any audience.

We're on our way – it's now time to locate and target your audience and to present them with a wealth of options for your products and services. In this chapter, we'll also look at how to structure your content into a *blended offering* that builds with and complements the relationship.

There has never been a better time to market yourself and your products.

Two Bites of the Apple

The immediacy and reach of the internet means that you now have two clear business avenues where previously you only had one.

1. Naturally, you still have the traditional ways of influencing your target audience face-to-face; once you have acquired your target audience through face-to-face and online networking and word of mouth, you can run live seminars

and workshops, which are still unbeatable for building relationships and maximising your impact.

2. In addition, you can now offer them the modern approach: a suite of online products, such as podcasts, audio CDs and audiobooks, online audio-visual workshops, plus live online seminars for large groups of paying customers. The impact may not be as powerful as in a face-to-face live session, but the results and the value of online interactive products is still impressive and represents a huge opportunity.

The opportunity is here for anyone with his or her own message to package their products and services in a variety of different ways, which will accommodate any learning scenario or preferred learning style.

Physical products

As far as products are concerned, the great thing about having a physical offering is that you are providing a viable learning alternative to those members of your audience who cannot spare the time, are not available, or prefer to start their relationship with you from the privacy of their own home.

There are a couple of brilliant advantages to producing products:

- Once you have designed and built them, your job is done – it's a great way of building your brand and spreading your message

- Another great plus of having physical products is that they are transferrable; if you are doing your job, you will have produced some terrific content that will have inspired your original customer so much that word of mouth will kick in as well as the borrowing of your material by others, or at the least, a recommendation to others that they also invest in your material

Online and face-to-face services

As far as services are concerned, live events, whether at a bespoke live seminar or a workshop-styled learning intervention, are the main chances for you to influence large numbers of people at once.

Unlike the other options mentioned here, there is no substitute for an environment where you can express yourself in the moment and give your audience the live and full benefit of your knowledge and speaking experience. How you respond to questions and expound upon points raised is unique to *that* environment and *that* audience; it's your opportunity to shine.

Coupled with the relationship-building power of live interaction come a couple of great advantages.

1. As mentioned, public speaking has been labelled as mankind's greatest fear according to various surveys over the years. As a result, your standing in front of a live audience sends out a powerful message: that you are passionate enough about your subject to build a business and to 'step up' in a notoriously challenging environment to speak your message. It's a very powerful thing to do, it's not for the faint-hearted. As a result, you will inspire and attract like-minded people, the kind of customers you want, from whom you can learn as much as you teach.

2. You may remember my description of my early days in the speaking business. I described in some detail the high-stakes situations I was forced into. You are not going to be asked to stretch yourself in that way. Public speaking is one thing, public speaking whilst getting people to perform mind over matter experiences that even *you* haven't seen is quite another. I lived through it unscathed and you will too. And here's the thing: it really doesn't take long before you become used to doing it. The fear and apprehension goes away, to be replaced by excitement and an acute awareness of your personal power.

It's an endlessly explored topic – the fact that your confidence and self-belief will flourish and grow exponentially as a result of toughening yourself in a pressurised environment.

This will naturally depend upon your area of expertise and the offering you have in mind, but if possible, the recommendation is that you think about both options in a *blended offering* of both online and face-to-face content.

Make a name for yourself

Because of the massive technological leaps made over the last decade and the reconditioning of the human race from a 'paper and footsteps' to the savvy, digital, Facebook-led culture we see today, where no holds are barred and you can make billions of people aware of you within hours, the possibilities and opportunities of producing easy to access, easy to teach and to apply products and services at very little cost are endless.

There are no more excuses for *not* positioning yourself and your products in front of the audience you want! All you need to do is to look online for a wealth of great value service providers whose products will enable you to package and promote your offering in a highly efficient, mechanised manner and all from your laptop.

These options include any number of online products and services, software tools to organise and manage your database of customers, and a website, either hosted or self-built, to create a learning hub, a power base, a reference library, a meeting point and a marketing engine all rolled into one.

So let's see what you can put together in a little more detail. I will look at two elements here: the 'what' – your offering itself and the 'how' – your methodology and some ideas for promotion.

1. The WHAT

Online offering: audio products

As we all know, the audiobook is fast overtaking the paper alternative, largely due to the ease of access and to the mobility provided by modern mobile phones which can carry hundreds of unabridged audio files. In addition, there is a growing trend in today's insane traffic for individuals to use commuting time or regular driving obligations for serious learning. The phrase 'mobile training room' when applied to the car is a very recent arrival and it points to the way the future is shaping. Audio programmes can either take the form of downloadable podcasts or audio CDs – a great physical product that provides huge flexibility for the user in that they can be used either in-car or in-home.

Online offering: audio-visual programmes

This is particularly effective if you have content to deliver that has any level of detail involved. The idea behind screen capture is that you can speak and present as you would in any online event, but your slides are also available. So in effect, this means that when you need to explain a concept, you can introduce the concept, open the slide and explain the concept as you reveal the various elements of the slide as you go. You can then make the slides available afterwards as a value-add for your delegates.

Online offering: webinars

The great thing about online webinars is flexibility. These audio-visual broadcasts are terrific because thousands of participants can watch and participate interactively at the same time. You can also pre-record these so that although they sound 'live' you can then offer your customers other opportunities to log on and benefit from your insights and content at their leisure.

After a simple registration process, your target audience can watch the webinar from any location, at any time, and on any device. The results are measurable thanks to the large amount of data that is collected prior to, during and after the webinar.

Online offering: membership programmes

In many ways, the online membership model is unbeatable as what could be called a 'banker' product. The rationale behind this is simple: you are looking to serve your members with great value at manageable cost. The idea is to present your online members with a learning platform that you release on a regular basis – either monthly if your content is detailed and requires practice or fortnightly, depending on your subject matter and technicality.

The value for them is that they get regular, bite-sized great content. The value for you as the provider is that you can record a whole multi-module programme at one go, which means you can sit back and relax as far as one of your central products is concerned. Once it's done, it's done.

Face-to-face offering: training courses and workshops

Depending upon your offering, this will more than likely be the 'engine room' of your whole offering. This is where the most intensive learning environments will happen and where you get to share your core learning with an audience which has not only paid to be there but has also set a lot of valuable time aside as a priority to learn from your expertise. It's where you have built enough trust with your audience for them to commit to three or even four days of solid learning.

The advantage of this format is that your audience is not only benefiting from your training in the learning sense but they are also getting to practise what they have learnt in an atmosphere of support and feedback. It's also where your brand will either grow and flourish or alternatively scrape by, depending upon the experience your delegates have in the room over this time and their levels of perceived value as a result.

Face-to-face offering: ongoing mentoring

The group-mentoring element of your offering is very much aimed at the higher end of your membership. What is meant by this is that what you are offering is a much more forensic approach to your members' learning than the 'leave it to them' approach of the online membership or webinar products.

The process involves several meetings a year, each of which will focus on different elements of your content. The format should take the shape of the introduction of topics, followed by discussion and individual practice with group feedback. The individual intervention can also be filmed for retrospective learning.

Face-to-face offering: 1:2:1 coaching

Individual 1:2:1 coaching, offered on either a half-day or a full-day basis, demands lots of your precious time. It's the pinnacle of your offering and the price should reflect that.

Anthony Robbins makes no bones about the fact that he will put his prospective 1:2:1 'coachees' through hoops, in an attempt to ensure that they really are committed to change. Only when they have proved their commitment will he then charge a premium price for his time.

You need to make your personal time aspirational. It goes without saying that your suite of products and services has already positioned you as an expert in your field and therefore your personal time is at a premium.

Your members have already benefited from huge amounts of varied content, based upon your specialist area, and because it's a numbers game, only the very committed, the very serious and the very high-profile individuals will be looking to take advantage of your personal time and attention. Have no fear though, if you have done your job, there will be a demand, even at multiple thousands of pounds a day.

Creating a community

Why not make the most of today's world, where you can blend both traditional methods of face-to-face communication with digital, targeted, easy to use online formats.

These can include:

- Blogs and e-books

- Free weekly tips

- Free online webinars

- Face-to-face keynotes, workshops and seminars

- Face-to-face elite coaching

As mentioned in this chapter, the key here is to remember that your audience, your members and customers are all individuals in their own right, who will have different preferences as to how they process information.

2. The HOW

Promotion

So we now know *what* to offer our clients, both online and face-to-face. The next step is to understand *how* to let the clients know that a) you exist and b) you have some life-enhancing offers for them.

Case study – advertising and database management

In the late 1990s, during the internet 'boom', I and an actor friend started an online portal for actors. Unfortunately, as with everything to do with the internet at the time, online advertising was not in place and, as a result, in order to attract a customer base I was compelled to take out a series of large, one-page advertisements in *The Stage* – the actors 'rag'. The cost was fist-bitingly steep and, in the end, the new customers to my website were not 'targeted' enough; that is to say, the advertisements had not been specific enough to attract precisely the community we were after.

The result? Huge cost and a mediocre rather diluted membership community.

So what's the new alternative?

Targeted advertising

The idea behind a multi-format offering is that you are living in both worlds: the new and the traditional. As far as the new world is concerned, much is now possible due to the advent of targeted advertising. It means that you can reach your target audience far more accurately than traditional methods of blanket advertising would allow and at a microscopic fraction of the price.

Traditional 'mainstream' advertising was – and still is – prohibitively expensive for individuals and remains the domain of the large, well-funded organisation. However, the internet age has brought great opportunities along with it in the shape of global networking and reference sites such as Facebook and YouTube, each of which has a staggering number of users. Because of modern data analytics software, these digital behemoths (Facebook, if a country, would now be the biggest in the world) are able to gain huge amounts of information about each user, which in turn allows the innovative internet marketeer to utilise the 'piggy-back' marketing approach, reaching highly specific, targeted demographics by region, age and industry.

This in turn means that, for the first time, you are a) taking the guesswork out of your advertising efforts and b) using an infrastructure that has already done most of the work for you. Moreover, the advertising options are on a pay per click basis, which means that unless someone accesses your advertisement, you don't pay.

The statistics speak for themselves:

- 78% of small businesses attract new customers and engage current ones using social media

- 71% of consumers who experience positive social media care are likely to recommend that brand to others

The power of influence

A great definition of influence goes as follows: 'The art of letting *other* people have *your* way.'

There is a voluntary journey implied here that speaks of showing your commitment and quality to others so that they can then join you because you have demonstrated your promise.

Persuasion and manipulation, however, are very different; these two words conjure up the hard sell, the bamboozle, the arm-lock 'if you want this, you have to do *this*' etc. Relationship is not necessary with these.

This is reminiscent of subscription-based TV for example, where, if you want to watch a certain programme, you have to pay the expensive fees that your TV company has secured by means of exclusive rights to that programme or filmed event. If you want to watch it, you have to pay.

Influence then is very different from persuasion or manipulation. Influence requires a) time and b) a relationship to form. The pay-offs are of course enormous. People will trust you and will be loyal as a result.

In this instance, the electronics giant Apple springs to mind. The vast majority of iPhone, Mac or iPad users are not financially compelled by Apple in the same way as the TV station example, but they are (and the stats back this up conclusively) far more likely to remain loyal to the brand because they feel that they are 'Apple people'. The thought of switching brands is unthinkable because they associate themselves with the avant-garde, sexy, intuitive products provided.

So what does this mean for you and the marketing of your products and services?

Give first

In the early days of the internet, the recognised approach was to ask your prospective customers to sign up to your website, in order to enjoy the products/information/services that you were looking to promote. Once they had signed on the dotted electronic line, you could then start to offer them value for their commitment. It made perfect sense – you work behind the scenes to give people highly attractive benefits and then offer these benefits in return for their membership. Sometimes this would include a membership fee, which would constitute the 'meat and potatoes' of your income. You might offer extra levels or tiers of membership at a premium on top of this. Alternatively, you might offer free membership with a range of paid products and services on the side.

Things have changed however. The plus side of a global audience at your fingertips still remains, but the fierce competition and the resulting choice now offered to any interested punter in any market sector means that your prospective customers have become a) fickle and easily bored or distracted and b) choosy!

As a result, the savvy internet marketeer has now realised that the old ways aren't going to get the job done in the same way as they used to. In order to stay ahead of the game in an astonishingly fast-changing environment, you have to offer the value first and then ask your prospective customer to sign up.

Free content is now the name of the game, in order to influence and then to create the beginnings of a relationship with your target audience. The aim is to give your target audience a high-quality free product that will give value and encourage them to sign up at the same time. The pressure is off because at this stage you are not asking them for anything except their details.

Education is the answer

Possibly the best advice is to remember that the word 'sales' tends to stimulate strong negative impulses because, as we learned in the piece around beliefs, what you believe affects your emotions, behaviour and results. As a result, the negative beliefs we have as humans with sales create emotional responses that cause us to 'shut off' in the same automatic way that we slam our foot on the brake pedal when we see the lights changing to red.

It's automatic: 'sales are bad, so I'm not interested.'

Think about it: whenever you hear the doorbell ring and you open your door to see a complete stranger on your doorstep, your initial emotion is negative and your behaviour follows accordingly; it's, at best, a firmly shut door in the face.

This makes selling, either online or face-to-face, a real challenge. If people want to buy and they are looking online for what you are offering, then you may well be lucky. If, however, you are in a very competitive market and are pitching your products and services, it's a potential minefield and can be dispiriting. Not only are you trying to convert sales in the face of scepticism at best and cynicism at worst, you are also one of many looking to win people over.

The answer? As with most of the really great lessons to be learnt in this industry, it's a shift in mindset.

Instead of giving yourself the mental uphill slog of converting sales, with the pressure of losing if you don't succeed, try and see your sales approach as teaching and inspiring learners. Remember, no one likes to lose but everyone likes to learn. If you focus on the process, the results will take care of themselves.

Here's some social proof: Tony Hsieh, the American online entrepreneur and founder of Zappos, famously quoted, *'Chase the vision, not the money and the money will end up following you.'*

A recommendation is for you to put sales *per se* out of your head altogether. If you get your products and services right and you make sure that they are both innovative and useful, your last task is to make sure that people know you exist, and with consistency and persistence you will get there.

So how does the concept of sales into education actually work?

A functional website

The most important thing you will need is a simple yet functional website – a hub where anyone looking to access your products and services can go. There are two main functions that your website will need to accommodate.

1. Online membership with database management

Going back to my earlier example about my actors website in the 1990's, the second big challenge was the lamentable fact that we had not fine-tuned and checked our website enough to handle the database management.

Granted, the internet as anything other than a reference tool was still new, but still, the incoming members, such as they were, had persistent challenges with signing up, and for every ten new members we had two or three emails complaining of not being able to access the members' area or the opt-in page. This was 'the school of hard knocks' where as innovators in a new space we were discovering first hand just how problematic the 'wonderful' new age of information and technology could be.

Hindsight is a wonderful thing and, as a result, getting the basics right is at least as important as 'wowing' your members with all your fantastic material.

So, to basics, and there is nothing new about online membership and yet it remains a tried and tested means of:

- Creating a loyal following

- Capturing and nurturing a growing database

- Ensuring customer service

- Offering deals and discounts

- Sharing best practice and thought leadership

- Creating a sense of community

It also gives you a sense of control as the generator of an online community in that you can manage the expectations, both of your online audience and of your returns, based upon the size and response of your community.

There are many terrific do-it-yourself websites available for the modern entrepreneur, which are easy to design and build the fundamental elements you will need if you wish to combine your face-to-face element with online products and services. It's a rapidly changing world, but as this is written, Kajabi is very popular and there are other good options out there as well, such as Ruzuku, WizIQ and Academy of Mine, which are ridiculously good value for money, highly functional and you can customise them according to your market, audience, required functionality and personal preferences. Some have free hosting with a commission-based fee structure; others host your site with a monthly fee.

For example, for a manageable hosting fee per month, you can:

- Design your own theme, using very easy, intuitive guided processes – you don't even need to know about design

- Market up to 100 products

- Deliver up to 40,000 marketing emails a month

- Cater for approximately 10,000 members (more for a fee)

- Host different websites if you have different 'arms' to your business under the same umbrella site, with up to 100 landing pages

- Send out automated 'drip feed' emails to people who have purchased from your site

- Benefit from limitless technical help

So, all in all, it's a very different world from when it began – and what's more, time has ironed out the glitches. It's very rare to encounter technical problems these days because the competition between these companies is so fierce that they can't afford to get any bad press – which is great news for you the consumer!

2. Merchant account

Along with the many hosted build-it-yourself website products available comes the option to purchase merchant capability, which is naturally a must-have option if you are looking to sell your online products and services. It's a simple matter of a couple of clicks to set up payment capability, which will enable you to receive payments from all around the world. The added bonus of a hosted product also means that you don't have to get involved with payment gateways which can be a little complicated.

As well as the thoughts above, you need to align your mindset to the concept of a *relationship* rather than an *encounter*. As a result, your approach needs to be structured rather than random. As reiterated throughout this book, you need to plan your relationship from your customer's perspective in a strategic rather than a tactical way.

It's a build, so therefore a process for creating a database of motivated customers might look something like this:

Free content: you can do a sequence of these, each quite short – four minutes or so – incorporating tips and techniques that address a need.

A step change: the next step involves a small step up as you invite your new member to join an online event. This can be a webinar, a masterclass or other online content. The key to remember here is that you are slowly building the relationship and with it, trust. People will rarely be ready to buy straight away and therefore credibility is what you are looking to build by offering great value and overdelivering on your promise. At the end of your online event you may mention an offer, which is your first paid product.

From here, you are starting to build your relationship with your new member.

A final point.

The Magic of You

People often get it wrong – they try and sell *just* the product. Of course the product is the item in question, but you are the vehicle – the catalyst. Your online masterclass is the first opportunity that your potential customers will have to experience you 'live'. So the call to action is all about getting people to meet you face–to–face.

And ultimately... just remember that *you* are the best visual aid! Your face-to-face opportunity is where you get people to *like* your products and services – and to *love* you.

So, what now?

A challenge for you. It's the easiest thing in the world to theorise about challenges that we face when making career moves. Most of what we have looked at through the course of this book is self-evident – common sense in fact. Hopefully, by the time you reach this page you will be very clear about the much-repeated mantra throughout the book, that common sense is not common practice.

The Shift to Common Practice

Statistically, the point where theory turns to practice is the biggest stumbling block of all, for obvious reasons. It's hard to do. It's *really* hard to do – in practice you need to move from your comfort zone into what is commonly called the danger zone but what you could instead call the zone of opportunity.

This is where it is edgy, of course, but this is also where creativity happens and where you can become great – differentiated and a pioneer. Just look at some quotes from famous leaders in their field:

'Life is either a daring adventure or nothing at all' – Helen Keller

'If you aren't in over your head, how do you know how tall you are?' – TS Eliot

'I don't run away from a challenge because I am afraid. Instead, I run towards it, because the only way to escape fear is to trample it beneath your foot' – Nadia Comaneci

'Our very survival depends upon our ability to stay awake, to adjust to new ideas, to remain vigilant and to face the challenge of change' – Martin Luther King Jr

'Hope and change are hard-fought things' – Michelle Obama

'A challenge only becomes an obstacle when you bow to it' – Ray Davis

There are lessons here. In a nutshell – it's hard, but it's *possible*.

There are two things that you will need above all.

Self-awareness

We have looked at the autopilot and the term self-awareness many times during the course of these chapters. Self-awareness is the cornerstone of learning and will make the difference between your success and your struggle. Unless you can remain vigilant and measure your progress in all the chapters mentioned above, you will not reap the benefits of your efforts.

Self-awareness is a discipline. It's not hard, it's more a matter of engraining a habit that will support and sustain you, so remember your *rejoice, reframe, refine* journal – it's the best tip you can give yourself.

Self-reliance

The last attribute that you need in order to succeed beyond your wildest expectations in this area is self-reliance. The dictionary describes self-reliance as '*a dependence upon one's own resources*', which is fine.

More emotive and for many, a guide for life, is the epic poem '*If*'. Here are a couple of key lines:

If you can meet with Triumph and Disaster

And treat those two impostors just the same;

This poem by Rudyard Kipling sums up self-reliance. Whilst it is dramatic, we are talking about a dramatic life skill here: the power to communicate with impact from a place of which this poem positively *screams*:

Integrity and emotional control and strong will and steadfastness and courage and persistence and a sense of humour, both at ourselves as well as at the crazy journey of life itself.

In the context of public speaking, it is always prudent to remind oneself to expect the unexpected.

Mental preparation is a strategy that cannot be recommended highly enough. A great way of seeing this is as an 'accept and grow' technique. If you are facilitating with an audience renowned for its analytical or scrutinising reputation, the best way to approach these situations is to see any challenge, criticism or comment as a gift upon which to accept and to grow the conversation. Trust yourself! You know your stuff!

Summary

- We have covered the 'What' – a way in which to package your products and services

- We have also looked at the 'How' – some outline ideas into how you can promote your offering

- We have looked at several different ways of packaging your products and services that will appeal to the varying demands of your customers, whatever their learning preference

Epilogue

I truly believe that things in life happen for a reason.

In the last seven years, I have donned the mantle of freelance speaker and coach, specialising in providing solutions for organisations to industries ranging from banking and insurance to fashion, retail, IT and telecoms, and pharmaceuticals.

Throughout these seven years, I have travelled consistently – and for some reason far more abroad than here in the UK – to over 60 countries and every continent. In one notable year, I spent over 27 weeks abroad. It has been an extraordinary existence of living out of a suitcase and switching from one client to the next. And during this time, somehow, I seem to have just… carried on doing the job, without stopping to think *why* I have been putting myself through this for all this time.

As I sit in that lounge in San Francisco, I suddenly realise that the gentleman who is seated next to me wants to talk. He looks pleasant, and interested, as he asks, 'You look like you've done some travelling, where have you travelled from?' I tell him about my week.

And here's the thing: I am expecting him to say what everyone else says, i.e. 'Wow, how exciting, all that travel etc.,' but he doesn't. He sits there, looking out at the aircraft either landing or floating off into the blue, and after a long pause, he turns, smiles and says, 'You must be doing what you're doing for a very good reason.'

It's a defining moment.

I have been travelling for six days; I may have had as much as three hours' sleep a night at a pinch. Worse, I have been whizzing around 16 hours difference of time zones which has utterly confused my body clock, and I have delivered three keynote speeches to three different clients in three different continents.

I'm running on empty but in that moment I forget the exhaustion; I forget that years of global travel has taxed the relationships that matter to me most; I forget that I haven't seen nearly enough of my ten-year-old son during some very important years.

I realise that I *am* doing what I am doing for a good reason. Somewhere, I realise that I have always known this, but much as it *really* pains me to admit it, whilst I was a good professional actor, I know that I am a better speaker and that things are as they should be. I realise that the acting has been the preparation for what I do now.

I know that when I stand and deliver my speeches, the experience and the learning often makes a difference to the quality of people's lives. For many, my speeches are interesting and humorous and for some, who hear what I have to say at important or defining moments in their lives, I am lucky enough to witness real and lasting change in others for the better.

I get to see moments where people realise their potential, where they can see clarity of purpose and the excitement of the possibilities that this brings.

I realise that my purpose in life is to be a catalyst, an enabler, helping others to unlock their own potential.

And I realise – consciously for the first time – that I *am* here for a very good reason. I am doing what I was always meant to be doing. And it's only taken me 15 years to realise it!

But *what* a journey it has been.

Further Reading

For your audience

Michael Grinder – *The Science of Nonverbal Communication*

Robert Cialdini – *Influence - The Psychology of Persuasion*

Nancy Duarte – *Slide:Ology*

For your development

Stephen Covey – *The 7 Habits of Highly Successful People*

Anthony Robbins – *Awaken the Giant Within*

William Bridges – *Transitions*

Daniel Goleman – *Emotional Intelligence*

Robert Dilts – *Sleight of Mouth*

Dale Carnegie – *How to Win Friends and Influence People*

Simon Sinek – *Start with Why*

Susan Jeffers – *Feel the Fear and Do It Anyway*

Brené Brown – *Rising Strong*

For your marketing

Tim Hughes and Matt Reynolds – *Social Selling*

About the Author

Oliver Medill spent ten years as a professional actor (West End, TV and film) before entering the mentoring and coaching industry. One of the UK's leading communication coaches and speakers, he works both in the corporate field with senior executives and corporate teams as well as with individual professionals, entrepreneurs and media personalities.

When in the UK he lives in London.

www.allaboutimpact.co.uk

Hire me: speaker training, public speaking engagements

Since writing *The Impact Formula*, I have been contacted by many individuals wanting help with the design and delivery of their presentations and speeches, as well as organisations for speaking engagements at their conferences and for training of their senior executives, both in the UK and in the USA.

Services offered include:

- Speaker training for individuals

- Speaker training for groups

- Elite speaker tailored sessions for high stakes pitches, keynote speeches and C level presentations

If you would like more information, please visit the 'hire me' page at my website: www.allaboutimpact.co.uk

Or email me at: oliver@allaboutimpact.co.uk

I look forward to hearing from you!

Free Offer

One of the hardest skills to master is putting your speech or presentation together in the first place.

Where do you start? What's the first step? And the second, third, fourth and fifth for that matter?

There are so many variables and you have to make sure that you are planning each step empathically, i.e. from the audience's perspective – rather than just from your own.

It can be a daunting task and many are the times that I have sat in front of a blank PowerPoint screen wrestling with the challenge of constructing something that is worth listening to.

The answer?

It's called The Audience SOLVER.

The Audience SOLVER is what I designed as an antidote for all those frustrating (and wasted!) hours.

It's a series of simple, easy-to-use steps that will guide you through the process of planning and constructing presentations and speeches in a way that builds your case in a compelling and persuasive way.

If you use the Audience SOLVER, I can promise you that you will not be spending any more time wondering where the content is coming from.

Just enter this link online www.allaboutimpact.co.uk/solver and I'll instantly share this powerful planning tool with you.

You'll love it!

Oliver Medill

www.allaboutimpact.co.uk